I0358319

بِسْمِ اللَّهِ الرَّحْمَٰنِ الرَّحِيمِ

In the name of Allah, The All-Merciful,
The Kindest towards believers.

Disclaimer

Contact : Admin@islamiclessonsmadeeasy.com.au

Visit us :

- Facebook.com/islamiclessonsmadeeasy
- Youtube.com/islamiclessonsmadeeasy
- Instagram.com/islamic_lessons_me
- Islamiclessonsmadeeasy.com.au
- Ilme.net.au

The pictures used are the property of Islamic Lessons Made Easy. The content and rulings are taken from various leading scholars and are presented in a simplified manner. Therefore, for the exact definition and explanation, please refer to the original sources.

First Edition

Contents

Transliteration	4
Introduction	5
Ṣalāt al-Āyāt	6
Ṣalāt al-Ghufaylah	29
Ṣalāt Jaʿfar al-Ṭayyār	41
Ṣalāt al-Eid	71
Ṣalāt al-Waḥshah	83
Nawāfil prayers	92
Nāfilah of ʿIshāʾ prayer	95
Nāfilah of Layl	102
Ṣalāt al-Shafʿ	109
Ṣalāt al-Witr	115
Glossary	123

Transliteration

ا	a
ب	b
ت	t
ث	th
ج	j
ح	ḥ
خ	kh
د	d
ذ	dh
ر	r
ز	z
س	s
ش	sh
ص	ṣ
ض	ḍ
ط	ṭ
ظ	ẓ
ع	ʿ
غ	gh
ف	f
ق	q
ك	k
ل	l
م	m
ن	n
ه	h
و	w
ي	y
ـَا / ىٰ / آ	ā
ـِي	ī
ـُو	ū

ʾ - Read with a sudden pause of air.

(saw) - Blessings of Allah be upon him and his family.

(n) - Better not to pronounce it. But if you do pronounce it, you do not pronounce the letter after it.

(as) - Peace be upon him/them.

(swt) - Glorious and Exalted Is He.

Introduction

﴿ إِنَّ الصَّلَاةَ تَنْهَىٰ عَنِ الْفَحْشَاءِ وَالْمُنكَرِ وَلَذِكْرُ اللَّـهِ أَكْبَرُ ﴾

Verily prayer keeps (one) away from indecency and evil, and certainly the remembrance of Allah is greater. (29:45)

The Holy Prophet (saw) said:

"If there is a stream (of water) at the door of the house of one of you where he washes himself five times a day, will there be any dirt on your body?"

He was answered: "No".

Then he (saw) said:

"Indeed, the example of the prayer is like the example of the flowing stream. Whenever he keeps up prayer, the sins he has committed between two ritual prayers will be vanished."
(*Wasāil al-Shīʿah,* v.3, p.7)

How to Pray
Ṣalāt al - Āyāt

2 x *rakʿahs*

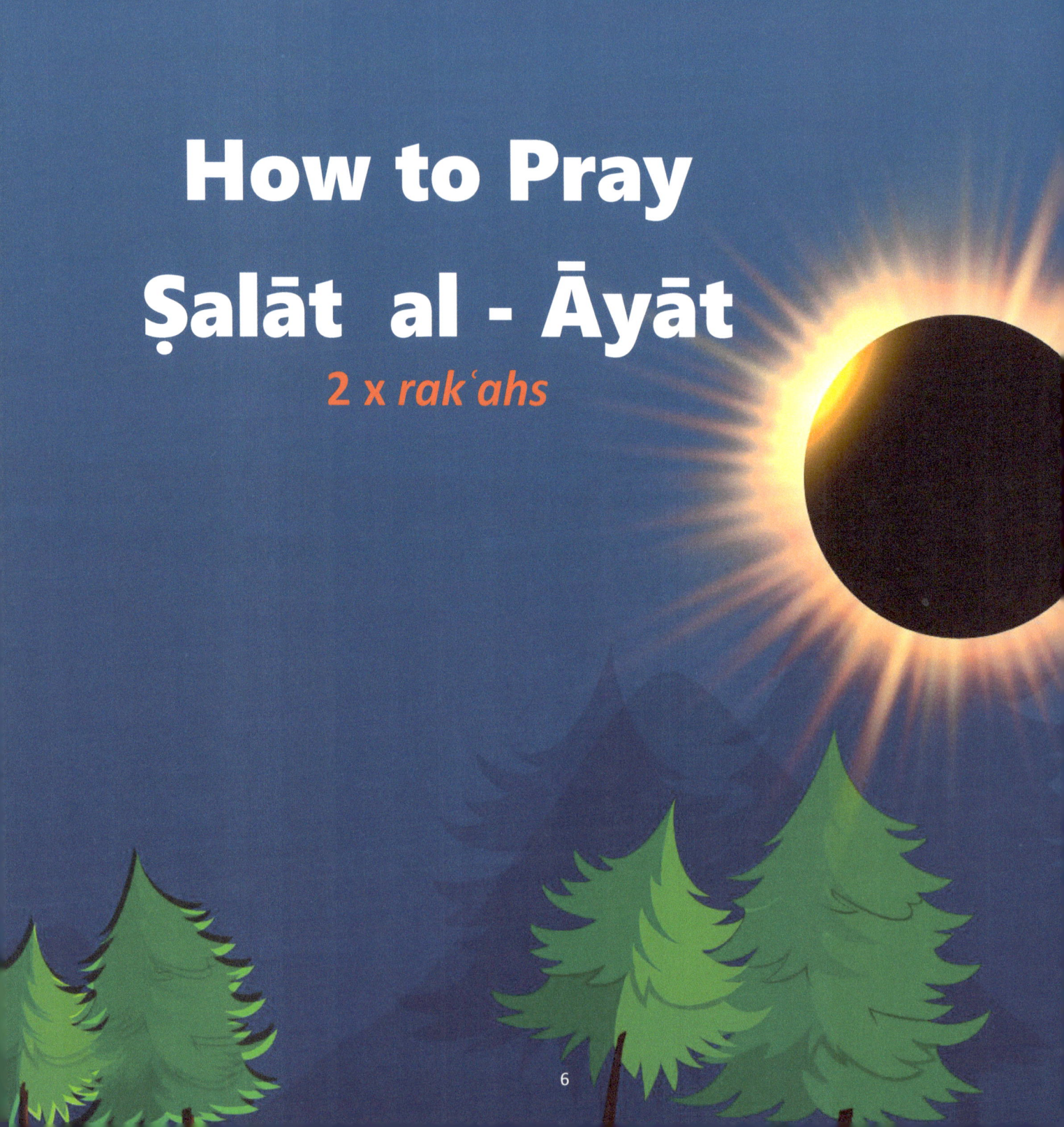

In the past, some people believed in superstitions when certain natural events occurred. For example, when Ibrahim, the son of the Prophet Muḥammad (saw), passed away at a young age, a solar eclipse happened, and people thought it was because of Ibrahim's death.

When the Prophet Muḥammad (saw) heard this, he stood up, praised God, and said, "**Solar and lunar eclipses are signs of God and do not occur because of someone's death. When they happen, you should offer a prayer**."

This prayer is called *Ṣalāt al-Āyāt*. In Arabic, "*Āyāt*" is the plural form of "*Āyah*", which means a sign. This prayer is named *Āyāt* because it is performed when certain natural events occur, acknowledging these events as signs of God's power and not superstitions.

It is obligatory for all sane Muslim men and women who have reached the age of Islamic maturity to pray *Ṣalāt al-Āyāt* if the conditions are met.

This prayer is obligatory when there is a solar or lunar eclipse even if the eclipse is partial or if there is an earthquake, with the obligation applying only to those in the affected area, not elsewhere.

The time for performing *Ṣalāt al-Āyāt* during a solar or lunar eclipse starts when the eclipse begins and continues until the sun or moon returns to its normal state. However, if the eclipse is over, the prayer becomes *qaḍāʾ* (a missed prayer that should be made up).

The prayer consists of 2 *rakʿahs*, and in each *rakʿah*, there are 5 *rukūʿs*, totaling 10 *rukūʿs*. There are two methods, short and long, for performing the prayer, but we will demonstrate the shorter method.

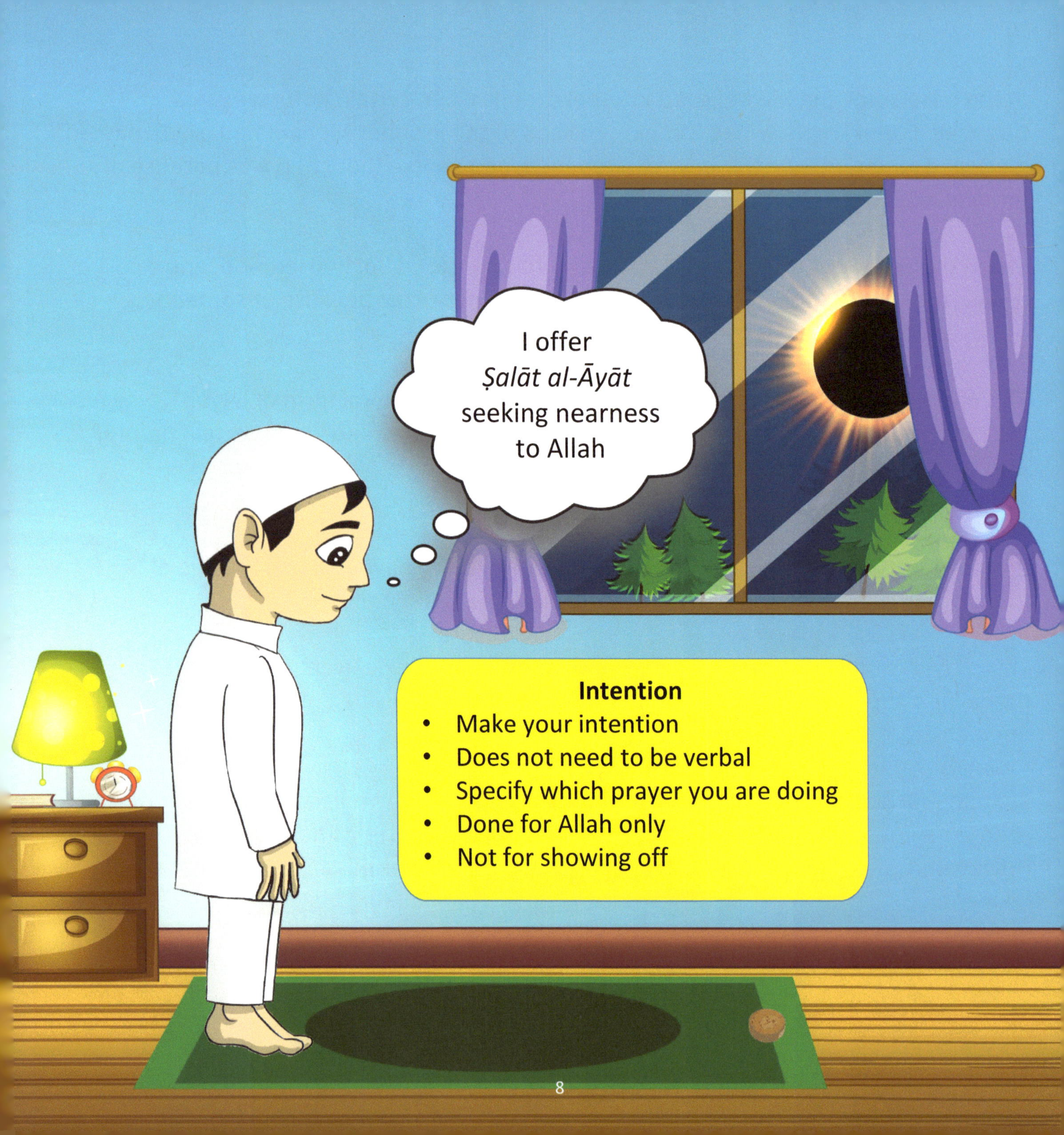

Intention

- Make your intention
- Does not need to be verbal
- Specify which prayer you are doing
- Done for Allah only
- Not for showing off

Lift both hands up to your ears and say *Allahu Akbar*
(Allah is greater than what He is described as)

Allahu Akbar

- Must be pronounced at the beginning of every prayer
- Must be pronounced in correct Arabic
- Body must be still
- Recommended to raise hands to ears

- Remain standing
- Recite Sūrah al-Fātiḥah

بِسْمِ اللَّـهِ الرَّحْمَـٰنِ الرَّحِيمِ

Bismil lāhir Raḥmānir Raḥīm

I start in the name of Allah, The All-Merciful, The Kindest towards believers.

الْحَمْدُ لِلَّـهِ رَبِّ الْعَالَمِينَ

Alḥamdu lillāhi Rabbil ʿālamīn

All praise and thanks are (just) for Allah, The Nurturer of all worlds.

الرَّحْمَـٰنِ الرَّحِيمِ

Arraḥmānir Raḥīm

The All-Merciful, The Kindest towards believers.

مَالِكِ يَوْمِ الدِّينِ

Māliki yawmid dīn

The (only real) Owner of everything (and the only authority) on Judgement day.

إِيَّاكَ نَعْبُدُ وَإِيَّاكَ نَسْتَعِينُ

Iyyāka naʿbudu wa iyyāka nastaʿīn

(O Allah!) You (and only You) we worship, and You (and only You) we seek help from (as the independent deity).

اهْدِنَا الصِّرَاطَ الْمُسْتَقِيمَ

Ihdinaṣ ṣirāṭal mustaqīm

Guide (and take) us to the Right Path.

صِرَاطَ الَّذِينَ أَنْعَمْتَ عَلَيْهِمْ
غَيْرِ الْمَغْضُوبِ عَلَيْهِمْ وَلَا الضَّالِّينَ

Ṣirāṭal ladhīna anʿamta ʿalayhim ghayril maghḍūbi ʿalayhim wa laḍ ḍāllīn

The path of those whom You have bestowed your Blessings upon, not of those who have earned Your wrath and not (of) those who have gone astray.

1st *rakʿah*

1st verse

- Now we choose a *Sūrah* and split it into 5 parts
- Note, reciting the '*bismillāh*' on its own will not count as one verse
- Recite the first verse with the '*bismillāh*'

بِسْمِ اللَّهِ الرَّحْمَٰنِ الرَّحِيمِ

Bismil lāhir Raḥmānir Raḥīm

I start in the name of Allah, The All-Merciful, The Kindest towards believers.

قُلْ أَعُوذُ بِرَبِّ الْفَلَقِ

Qul aʿūdhu birabbil falaq

Say: I seek protection with the Nurturer of the Daybreak.

1st *rakʿah*

- Perform the first *rukūʿ*
- While in this position recite a *dhikr* (glorification)
- Also recommended to say

اللَّهُمَّ صَلِّ عَلَى مُحَمَّدٍ وَآلِ مُحَمَّدٍ

Allahumma ṣalli ʿalā Muḥammadi(n)w wa āli Muḥammad

(O Allah, Bless Muḥammad and the progeny of Muḥammad)

Dhikr

سُبْحانَ رَبِّيَ ٱلْعَظِيمِ وَ بِحَمدِهِ

Subḥāna Rabbiyal ʿaẓīmi wa biḥamdih

I declare that my Great Nurturer is free from imperfections, and I do so by praising Him.

2nd verse

Stand up and recite the second verse

مِن شَرِّ مَا خَلَقَ

Min sharri mā khalaq

From the evil of which He has created.

1st *rak'ah*

2nd *rukūʿ*

Perform the second *rukūʿ*

Dhikr

سُبْحانَ رَبِّيَ ٱلْعَظِيمِ وَ بِحَمدِهِ

Subḥāna Rabbiyal ʿaẓīmi wa biḥamdih

I declare that my Great Nurturer is free from imperfections, and I do so by praising Him.

1st *rakʿah*

3rd verse

Stand up and recite the third verse

وَمِن شَرِّ غَاسِقٍ إِذَا وَقَبَ

Wa min sharri ghāsiqin idhā waqab

And from the evil of the dark night when it comes.

1st *rak'ah*

3rd *rukūʿ*

Perform the third *rukūʿ*

Dhikr

سُبْحَانَ رَبِّيَ ٱلْعَظِيمِ وَ بِحَمدهِ

Subḥāna Rabbiyal ʿaẓīmi wa biḥamdih

I declare that my Great Nurturer is free from imperfections, and I do so by praising Him.

1st *rakʿah*

4th verse

Stand up and recite the fourth verse

وَمِن شَرِّ النَّفَّاثَاتِ فِي الْعُقَدِ

Wa min sharrin naffāthāti fil ʿuqad

And from the evil of those who blow on knots.

1st *rakʿah*

Perform the fourth *rukūʿ*

Dhikr

سُبْحانَ رَبِّيَ ٱلْعَظِيمِ وَ بِحَمدِهِ

Subḥāna Rabbiyal ʿaẓīmi wa biḥamdih

I declare that my Great Nurturer is free from imperfections, and I do so by praising Him.

Stand up and recite the fifth verse

وَمِن شَرِّ حَاسِدٍ إِذَا حَسَدَ

Wa min sharri ḥāsidin idhā ḥasad

And from the evil of the envious (ones) when they envy.

1st rakʿah

Perform the fifth *rukūʿ*

Dhikr

سُبْحانَ رَبِّيَ ٱلْعَظيمِ وَ بِحَمدهِ

Subḥāna Rabbiyal ʿaẓīmi wa biḥamdih

I declare that my Great Nurturer is free from imperfections, and I do so by praising Him.

- Stand up straight and still
- Recommended to say
  Samiʿal lāhu liman ḥamidah
  (Allah hears the one who praises Him)

1st *rakʿah*

1st *sajdah*

- Place your forehead on the ground in humility
- Place both palms of your hands, both knees and both big toes on the ground
- Remain still
- Recite in correct Arabic
- While in this position recite a *dhikr* (glorification)
- Also recommended to say

اللّٰهُمَّ صَلِّ عَلَى مُحَمَّدٍ وَآلِ مُحَمَّدٍ

Allahumma ṣalli ʿala Muḥammadi(n)w wa āli Muḥammad

(O Allah, Bless Muḥammad and the progeny of Muḥammad)

Dhikr

سُبْحَانَ رَبِّيَ ٱلأَعْلَىٰ وَ بِحَمْدِهِ

Subḥāna Rabbiyal aʿlā wa biḥamdih

I declare that my Most High Nurturer is free from imperfections, and I do so by praising Him.

1st *rakʿah*

- After the 1st *sajdah*, it is recommended to sit with the top part of the right foot on the sole of the left foot
- Recommended to place hands on thighs
- Recommended to say *Allahu Akbar*

Perform the second *sajdah* in the same way as the first *sajdah*

2nd *sajdah*

Dhikr

سُبْحانَ رَبِّيَ ٱلاَعْلَىٰ وَ بِحَمدِهِ

Subḥāna Rabbiyal aʿlā wa biḥamdih

I declare that my Most High Nurturer is free from imperfections, and I do so by praising Him.

1st *rakʿah*

1st *rakʿah*

- Stand back up
- Perform this second *rakʿah* in the same way you performed the first *rakʿah*:
  1- Recite Sūrah al-Fātiḥah
  2- Choose a *Sūrah* and spilt it into five parts
  3- After each verse you perform one *rukūʿ*, in total five *rukūʿs*
  4- Perform the two *sajdahs*

2nd *rakʿah*

After the two *sajdahs* recite the *tashahhud* (testifying) and then recite *taslīm* (salutation)

Tashahhud

اشْهَدُ اَنْ لااِلٰهَ اِلاَّ اللهُ وَحْدَهُ لاشَرِيكَ لَهُ

Ashhadu a(n)l lā ilāha illa lāhu waḥdahu lā sharīka lah

I testify that there is no god but Allah, He is alone, for whom there is no partner.

وَ أَشْهَدُ أَنَّ مُحَمَّداً عَبْدُهُ وَ رَسُولُه

Wa ashhadu anna Muḥammadan ʿabduhu wa rasūluh

And I testify that Muḥammad is His servant and His messenger.

أَللّٰهُمَّ صَلِّ عَلىٰ مُحَمَّدٍ وَ آلِ مُحَمَّد

Allahumma ṣalli ʿalā Muḥammadi(n)w wa āli Muḥammad

O Allah! Bless Muḥammad and the progeny of Muḥammad.

Taslīm

اَلسَّلامُ عَلَيْكَ اَيُّها ٱلنَّبِیُّ وَ رَحْمَةُ اللهِ وَ بَرَكاتُه

Assalāmu ʿalayka ayyuhan nabiyyu wa raḥmatullāhi wa barakātuh

Peace be upon you O Prophet, and Allah's mercy and His blessings (be upon you too).

اَلسَّلامُ عَلَينا وَ عَلىٰ عِبادِ اللهِ الصّالِحِينَ

Assalāmu ʿalaynā wa ʿalā ʿibādillāhiṣ ṣaliḥīn

Peace be upon us and upon the righteous servants of Allah.

اَلسَّلامُ عَلَيْكُمْ وَ رَحْمَةُ اللهِ وَ بَرَكاتُه

Assalāmu ʿalaykum wa raḥmatul lāhi wa barakātuh

Peace be upon you all, and Allah's mercy and His blessings (be upon you too).

2nd *rakʿah*

Notes

It is recommended that one performs *qunūt* before the 2nd, 4th, 6th, 8th and 10th *rukūʿ*, and if one performs *qunūt* before only the 10th *rukūʿ*, it is sufficient.

If there is more than one phenomenon where you must pray *Ṣalāt al Āyāt*, you must pray for each of them. For example, if there is a solar eclipse and an earthquake, one must perform two *Ṣalāt al-Āyāts*.

How to Pray Ṣalāt al – Ghufaylah

2 x *rakʿahs*

Ṣalāt al-Ghufaylah is one of the well-known *mustaḥab* (recommended) prayers and is prayed at the first part of the night right between *Maghrib* and *'Ishā'* prayers.

This period is known as the period of negligence i.e. *ghaflah*.

The word *Ghufaylah* (غُفَيلَة) is derived from the word *ghaflah* (غَفلَة) which means inattentiveness, heedlessness or neglect. Meaning forgetting about Allah, forgetting about one's duties to Allah.

If you committed a sin or were not conscience of the presence of Allah, you are in a state of *ghaflah*.

Ṣalāt al-Ghufaylah is said to remove you from this state of *ghaflah* (heedlessness).

To perform *Ṣalāt al-Ghufaylah*, it is best to pray it right after the *Maghrib* prayers and before the *'Ishā'* prayers.

You are permitted to hold a book, phone, or similar device to read from while praying until the prayer is memorised.

I offer
Ṣalāt al-Ghufaylah
seeking nearness
to Allah

Lift both hands up to your ears and say *Allahu Akbar*
(Allah is greater than what He is described as)

- Remain standing
- Recite Sūrah al-Fātiḥah

بِسْمِ اللَّـهِ الرَّحْمَـٰنِ الرَّحِيمِ

Bismil lāhir Raḥmānir Raḥīm

I start in the name of Allah, The All-Merciful, The Kindest towards believers.

الْحَمْدُ لِلَّـهِ رَبِّ الْعَالَمِينَ

Alḥamdu lillāhi Rabbil ʿālamīn

All praise and thanks are (just) for Allah, The Nurturer of all worlds.

الرَّحْمَـٰنِ الرَّحِيمِ

Arraḥmānir Raḥīm

The All-Merciful, The Kindest towards believers.

مَالِكِ يَوْمِ الدِّينِ

Māliki yawmid dīn

The (only real) Owner of everything (and the only authority) on Judgement day.

إِيَّاكَ نَعْبُدُ وَإِيَّاكَ نَسْتَعِينُ

Iyyāka naʿbudu wa iyyāka nastaʿīn

(O Allah!) You (and only You) we worship, and You (and only You) we seek help from (as the independent deity).

اهْدِنَا الصِّرَاطَ الْمُسْتَقِيمَ

Ihdinaṣ ṣirāṭal mustaqīm

Guide (and take) us to the Right Path.

صِرَاطَ الَّذِينَ أَنْعَمْتَ عَلَيْهِمْ

غَيْرِ الْمَغْضُوبِ عَلَيْهِمْ وَلَا الضَّالِّينَ

Ṣirāṭal ladhīna anʿamta ʿalayhim ghayril maghḍūbi ʿalayhim wa laḍ ḍāllīn

The path of those whom You have bestowed your Blessings upon, not of those who have earned Your wrath and not (of) those who have gone astray.

1st *rakʿah*

Now recite the following verse (21:87-88):

وَ ذَا النُّونِ إِذْ ذَهَبَ مُغَاضِباً فَظَنَّ أَن لَّن نَّقْدِرَ عَلَيْهِ فَنَادىٰ
فِي الظُّلُمَاتِ أَن لَّآ إِلٰهَ إِلاَّ أَنْتَ سُبْحَانَكَ إِنِّي كُنْتُ مِنَ
الظَّالِمِينَ (٨٧) فَاسْتَجَبْنَا لَهُ وَ نَجَّيْنَاهُ مِنَ الْغَمِّ وَ كَذٰلِكَ
نُنْجِي الْمُؤْمِنِينَ (٨٨)

Wa dhan nūni idh dhahaba mughāḍiban faẓanna a(n)l lan naqdira ʿalayhi fanādā fīẓ ẓulumāti a(n)l lā ilāha illā anta subḥānaka innī kuntu minaẓ ẓālimīn.
Fastajabnā lahu wa najjaynāhu minal ghammi wa kadhālika nunjil muʾminīn

And (O Messenger! Recall) ***dhan nūn*** (the whale resident) [Jonah], when he left (his people) in anger. So, he assumed that We would not be hard on him. However, (he went through the hardship and) while he was in the darkness (of the whale's stomach), he called out: "(O Allah! I testify that) there is no god except You; You are free from any deficiency and fault. Indeed, it was me who was one of the unjust ones".
So, We answered his prayers and saved him from that grief. And that is how We save the believers.

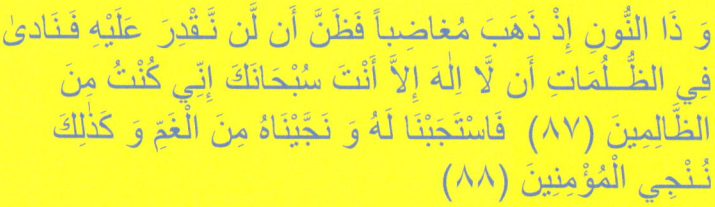

1st *rakʿah*

Perform the *rukūʿ* and the two *sajdahs*

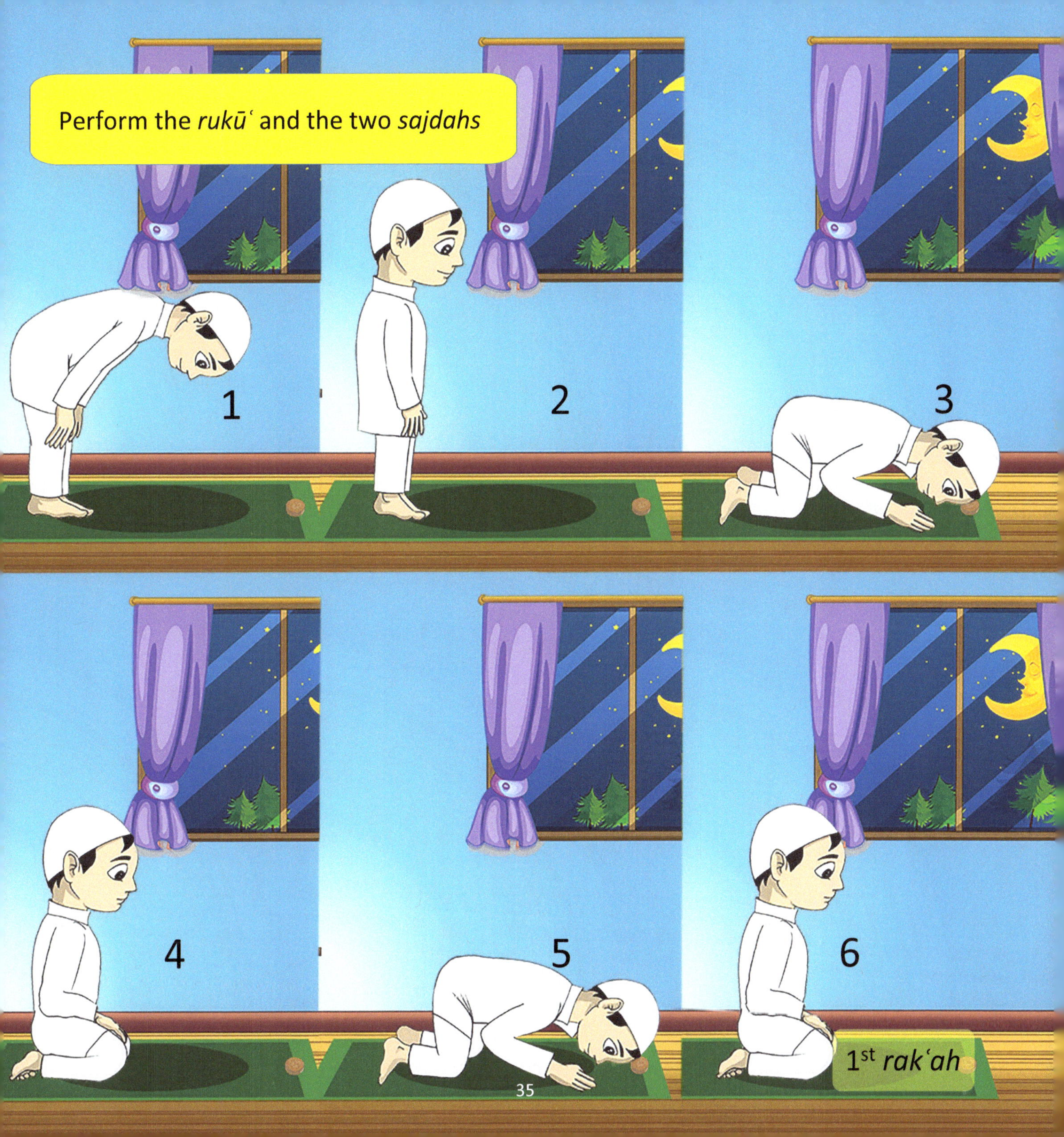

- Stand back up for the second *rakʿah*
- Recite Sūrah al-Fātiḥah

بِسْمِ اللَّـهِ الرَّحْمَـٰنِ الرَّحِيمِ

Bismil lāhir Raḥmānir Raḥīm

I start in the name of Allah, The All-Merciful, The Kindest towards believers.

الْحَمْدُ لِلَّـهِ رَبِّ الْعَالَمِينَ

Alḥamdu lillāhi Rabbil ʿālamīn

All praise and thanks are (just) for Allah, The Nurturer of all worlds.

الرَّحْمَـٰنِ الرَّحِيمِ

Arraḥmānir Raḥīm

The All-Merciful, The Kindest towards believers.

مَالِكِ يَوْمِ الدِّينِ

Māliki yawmid dīn

The (only real) Owner of everything (and the only authority) on Judgement day.

إِيَّاكَ نَعْبُدُ وَإِيَّاكَ نَسْتَعِينُ

Iyyāka naʿbudu wa iyyāka nastaʿīn

(O Allah!) You (and only You) we worship, and You (and only You) we seek help from (as the independent deity).

اهْدِنَا الصِّرَاطَ الْمُسْتَقِيمَ

Ihdinaṣ ṣirāṭal mustaqīm

Guide (and take) us to the Right Path.

صِرَاطَ الَّذِينَ أَنْعَمْتَ عَلَيْهِمْ

غَيْرِ الْمَغْضُوبِ عَلَيْهِمْ وَلَا الضَّالِّينَ

Ṣirāṭal ladhīna anʿamta ʿalayhim ghayril maghḍūbi ʿalayhim wa laḍ ḍāllīn

The path of those whom You have bestowed your Blessings upon, not of those who have earned Your wrath and not (of) those who have gone astray.

Now recite the following verse (6:59):

وَ عِنْدَهُ مَفَاتِحُ الْغَيْبِ لَا يَعْلَمُهَا إِلاَّ هُوَ وَ يَعْلَمُ مَا فِي الْبَرِّ
وَ الْبَحْرِ وَ مَا تَسْقُطُ مِن وَّرَقَةٍ إِلاَّ يَعْلَمُهَا وَ لاَ حَبَّةٍ فِي
ظُلُمَاتِ الْأَرْضِ وَ لاَ رَطْبٍ وَّ لاَ يَابِسٍ إِلاَّ فِي كِتَابٍ مُّبِينٍ

Wa ʿindahu mafātiḥul ghaybi lā yaʿlamuhā illā huwa wa yaʿlamu mā fil barri wal baḥri wa mā tasquṭu mi(n)w waraqatin illā yaʿlamuhā wa lā ḥabbatin fī ẓulumātil arḍi wa lā raṭbi(n)w wa lā yābisin illā fī kitābi(n)m mubīn

And the keys to the unseen belong to Him, no one knows them other than Him. And He knows whatever is in the land and sea, and no leaf falls except He knows, and no grain in the darkness of the earth, nor anything wet or dry, except (it is recorded) in a distinct Book.

2nd *rakʿah*

- Now it is recommended to perform *qunūt*
- Recite the following
- In the ellipsis (……), one should ask for their needs to be fulfilled

اَللّٰهُمَّ إِنِّي أَسْأَلُكَ بِمَفَاتِحِ الْغَيْبِ الَّتِي لَا يعْلَمُهَا إلاَّ أَنْتَ، أَنْ
تُصَلِّـىَ عَلَىٰ مُحَمَّدٍ وَّ آلِ مُحَمَّدٍ، وَ أَنْ تَـفْعَلَ بِي .....

Allāhumma innī as aluka bimafātiḥil ghaybil latī lā yaʿlamuhā illā ant, an tuṣalliya ʿalā muḥammadi(n)w wa āli muḥammad, wa an tafʿala bī ..... (ask for your needs)

O Allah! I ask You by the keys of the Unseen that no one knows except You, to bless Muḥammad and the progeny of Muḥammad and to fulfil for me ……. **(ask for your needs)**

Now recite the following:

اَللّٰهُمَّ أَنْتَ وِلِيُّ نِعْمَتِي وَ الْقَادِرُ عَلَىٰ طَلِبَتِي، تَعْلَمُ حَاجَتِي
فَأَسْأَلُكَ بِحَقِّ مُحَمَّدٍ وَّ آلِ مُحَمَّدٍ عَلَيْهِ وَ عَلَيْهِمُ السَّلَامُ، لَمَّا
قَضَيْتَهَا لِي

Allāhumma anta waliyyu niʿmatī wal qādiru ʿalā ṭalibatī, taʿlamu ḥājatī, fa as aluka bihaqqi muḥammadi(n)w wa āli muḥammadin ʿalayhi wa ʿalayhimus salām, lammā qaḍaytahā lī

O Allah! You are the Patron of my blessings and the One Powerful to respond to my request. You know my needs, so I ask You by the right of Muḥammad and the progeny of Muḥammad, peace be upon him and them, to fulfil them for me.

Perform the *rukūʿ* and the two *sajdahs*

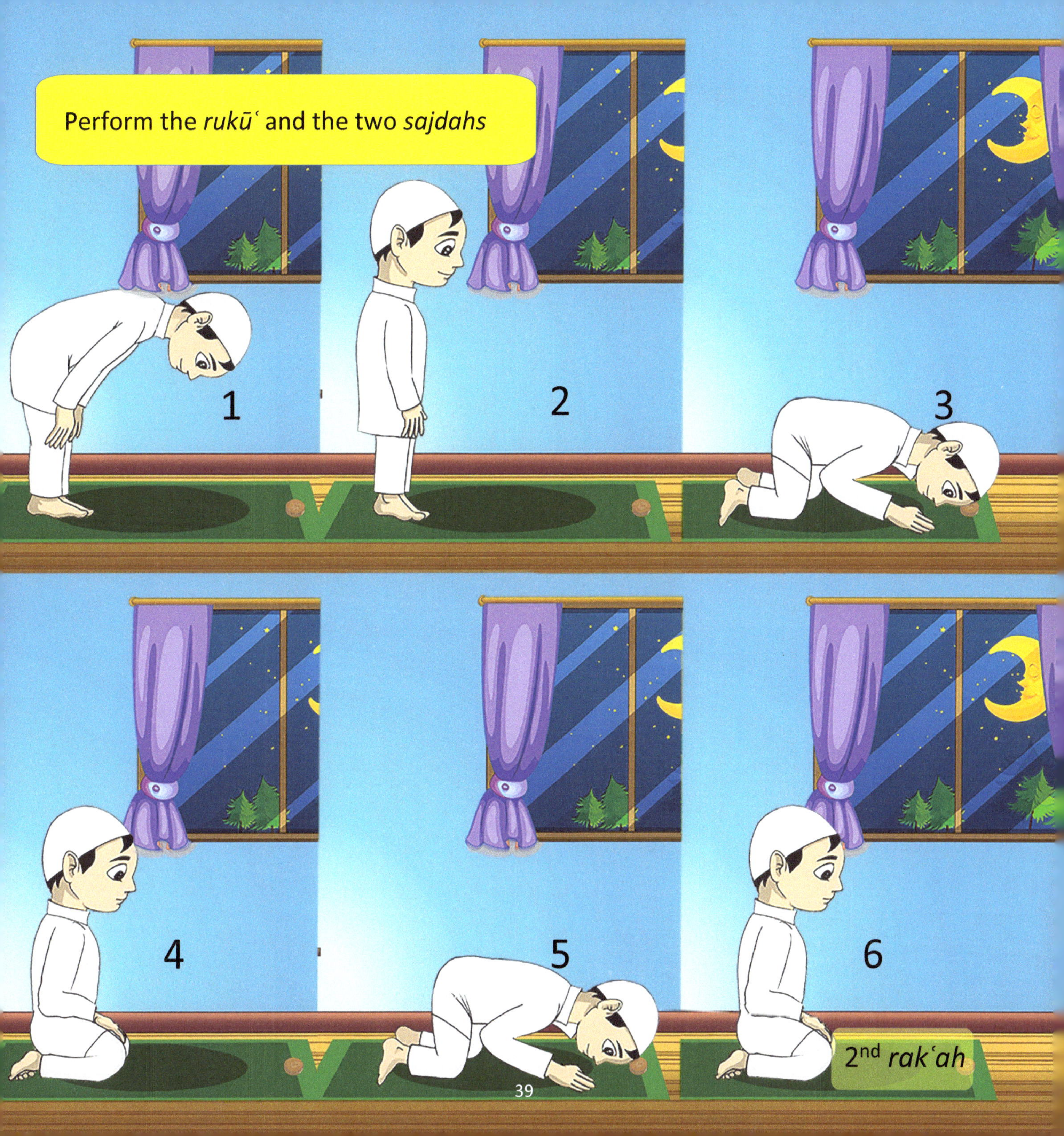

After the two *sajdahs* recite the *tashahhud* and then recite *taslīm*

Tashahhud

اشْهَدُ اَنْ لااِلٰهَ اِلاَّ اللهُ وَحْدَهُ لاشَرِيكَ لَهُ

Ashhadu a(n)l lā ilāha illa lāhu waḥdahu lā sharīka lah

I testify that there is no god but Allah, He is alone, for whom there is no partner.

وَ أَشْهَدُ أَنَّ مُحَمَّداً عَبْدُهُ وَ رَسُولُه

Wa ashhadu anna Muḥammadan ʿabduhu wa rasūluh

And I testify that Muḥammad is His servant and His messenger.

أَللّٰهُمَّ صَلِّ عَلىٰ مُحَمَّدٍ وَ آلِ مُحَمَّد

Allahumma ṣalli ʿalā Muḥammadi(n)w wa āli Muḥammad

O Allah! Bless Muḥammad and the progeny of Muḥammad.

Taslīm

اَلسَّلامُ عَلَيْكَ اَيُّها اَلنَّبِيُّ وَ رَحْمَةُ اللهِ وَ بَرَكاتُه

Assalāmu ʿalayka ayyuhan nabiyyu wa raḥmatullāhi wa barakātuh

Peace be upon you O Prophet, and Allah's mercy and His blessings (be upon you too).

اَلسَّلامُ عَلَينا وَ عَلىٰ عِبادِ اللهِ الصّالِحِينَ

Assalāmu ʿalaynā wa ʿalā ʿibādillāhiṣ ṣaliḥīn

Peace be upon us and upon the righteous servants of Allah.

السَّلامُ عَلَيْكُمْ وَ رَحْمَةُ اللهِ وَ بَرَكاتُه

Assalāmu ʿalaykum wa raḥmatul lāhi wa barakātuh

Peace be upon you all, and Allah's mercy and His blessings (be upon you too).

2nd *rakʿah*

How to Pray
Ṣalāt
Jaʿfar al – Ṭayyār

4 x *rakʿahs*

The prayer of *Jaʿfar al-Ṭayyār* is an important *mustaḥab* (recommended) prayer which is very rewarding. The prayer is recommended for forgiveness of one's sins and the divine response to one's needs and requests.

The Prophet Muḥammad (saw) taught this prayer to *Jaʿfar* the son of *Abū Ṭālib* upon his return from Abyssinia as a reward for the many years of patience there.

The prayer consists of 2 prayers with 2 *rakʿahs* in each prayer. That's 4 *rakʿahs* in total.

These 4 *tasbiḥs* are recited 75 times per *rakʿah*. So that's 300 times all up.

The best time to perform it is during the first hours of daylight before noon on Fridays.

If you don't have enough time to recite all the *tasbiḥs*, you can recite them after the prayer.

If some important issues arise, you can separate the two sets of prayers with a gap.

Tasbiḥ (Glorifications)

سُبْحَانَ اللهِ

Subḥān Allah

I declare that Allah is free from imperfections

وَ الْحَمْدُ لِلّٰهِ

Walḥamdu lillāh

And all praise is for Allah

وَ لاَ إِلٰهَ إِلاَّ اللهُ

Wa lā ilāha illal lāh

And there is no god but Allah

وَ اللهُ أَكْبَرُ

Wallahu Akbar

And Allah is greater (than what He is described as)

If you forget the *tasbiḥs* in a specific place you can make them up in another place. For example, if you missed the *tasbiḥ* in *rukūʿ* and then remember after raising your head, then you recite 20 *tasbiḥs* in that place, and so on.

If you don't know the complete *ṣūrahs* off by heart, you can hold a book to read off until you learn them.

• Make your intention
• Perform *Takbīrat al-iḥrām*
I offer *Ṣalāt*
Jaʿfar al-Ṭayyār
seeking nearness to Allah
Now say:
Allahu Akbar

- Remain standing
- Recite Sūrah al-Fātiḥah
- Now recite Sūrah al-Zalzalah once

بِسْمِ اللَّـهِ الرَّحْمَـٰنِ الرَّحِيمِ

Bismil lāhir Raḥmānir Raḥīm

I start in the name of Allah, The All-Merciful, The Kindest towards believers.

إِذَا زُلْزِلَتِ الْأَرْضُ زِلْزَالَهَا

Idhā zulzilatil arḍu zilzālahā

When the earth is shaken with its earthquake.

وَأَخْرَجَتِ الْأَرْضُ أَثْقَالَهَا

Wa akhrajatil arḍu athqālahā

And the earth discharges its burdens.

وَقَالَ الْإِنسَانُ مَا لَهَا

Wa qālal insānu mā lahā

And man says, "What is [wrong] with it?"

يَوْمَئِذٍ تُحَدِّثُ أَخْبَارَهَا

Yawma idhin tuḥaddithu akhbārahā

That Day, it will report its news.

بِأَنَّ رَبَّكَ أَوْحَىٰ لَهَا

Bi anna rabbaka awḥā lahā

Because your Nurturer has commanded it.

يَوْمَئِذٍ يَصْدُرُ النَّاسُ أَشْتَاتًا لِّيُرَوْا أَعْمَالَهُمْ

Yawma idhi(n)y yaṣdurun nāsu ashtāta(n)l li yuraw aʿmālahum

That Day, the people will depart separated [into categories] to be shown [the result of] their deeds.

فَمَن يَعْمَلْ مِثْقَالَ ذَرَّةٍ خَيْرًا يَرَهُ

Fama(n)y yaʿmal mithqāla dharratin khayra(n)y yarah

So whoever does an atom's weight of good will see it.

وَمَن يَعْمَلْ مِثْقَالَ ذَرَّةٍ شَرًّا يَرَهُ

Wama(n)y yaʿmal mithqāla dharratin sharra(n)y yarah

And whoever does an atom's weight of evil will see it.

1st *rakʿah*

Now recite 15 *tasbiḥs*

Tasbiḥ x 15

سُبْحَانَ اللهِ

Subḥān Allah

I declare that Allah is free from imperfections

وَ الْحَمْدُ لِلّٰهِ

Walḥamdu lillāh

And all praise is for Allah

وَ لاَ إِلٰهَ إِلاَّ اللهُ

Wa lā ilāha illal lāh

And there is no god but Allah

وَ اللهُ أَكْبَرُ

Wallahu Akbar

And Allah is greater (than what He is described as)

1st *rakʿah*

- Perform the *rukūʿ* and *dhikr*
- Now recite 10 *tasbiḥs*

Dhikr

سُبْحانَ رَبِّيَ ٱلْعَظِيمِ وَ بِحَمدهِ

Subḥāna Rabbiyal ʿaẓīmi wa biḥamdih

I declare that my Great Nurturer is free from imperfections, and I do so by praising Him.

Tasbiḥ x 10

سُبْحَانَ اللهِ

Subḥān Allah

I declare that Allah is free from imperfections

وَ الْحَمْدُ لِلهِ

Walḥamdu lillāh

And all praise is for Allah

وَ لاَ إِلهَ إِلاَّ اللهُ

Wa lā ilāha illal lāh

And there is no god but Allah

وَ اللهُ أَكْبَرُ

Wallahu Akbar

And Allah is greater (than what He is described as)

1st *rakʿah*

Stand up straight and recite 10 *tasbiḥs*

Tasbiḥ x 10

سُبْحَانَ اللهِ

Subḥān Allah

I declare that Allah is free from imperfections

وَ الْحَمْدُ لِلّهِ

Walḥamdu lillāh

And all praise is for Allah

وَ لاَ إِلَهَ إِلاَّ اللهُ

Wa lā ilāha illal lāh

And there is no god but Allah

وَ اللهُ أَكْبَرُ

Wallahu Akbar

And Allah is greater (than what He is described as)

1st *rakʿah*

- Perform the first *sajdah* and *dhikr*
- Now recite the *tasbiḥs* 10 times

1st *sajdah*

Dhikr

سُبْحَانَ رَبِّيَ ٱلأَعْلَىٰ وَ بِحَمدهِ

Subḥāna Rabbiyal aʿlā wa biḥamdih

I declare that my Most High Nurturer is free from imperfections, and I do so by praising Him.

Tasbiḥ x 10

سُبْحَانَ اللهِ

Subḥān Allah

I declare that Allah is free from imperfections

وَ الْحَمْدُ لِلّهِ

Walḥamdu lillāh

And all praise is for Allah

وَ لاَ إِلَهَ إِلاَّ اللهُ

Wa lā ilāha illal lāh

And there is no god but Allah

وَ اللهُ أَكْبَرُ

Wallahu Akbar

And Allah is greater (than what He is described as)

1st *rakʿah*

After the first *sajdah*, sit up and recite the *tasbiḥs* 10 times

Tasbiḥ **x 10**

سُبْحَانَ اللهِ

Subḥān Allah

I declare that Allah is free from imperfections

وَ الْحَمْدُ لِلّهِ

Walḥamdu lillāh

And all praise is for Allah

وَ لاَ إِلٰهَ إِلاَّ اللهُ

Wa lā ilāha illal lāh

And there is no god but Allah

وَ اللهُ أَكْبَرُ

Wallahu Akbar

And Allah is greater (than what He is described as)

1st *rakʿah*

2nd *sajdah*

- Perform the second *sajdah* in the same way as the first *sajdah*
- Now recite the *tasbiḥs* 10 times

Dhikr

سُبْحانَ رَبِّيَ ٱلأَعْلىٰ وَ بِحَمدِهِ

Subḥāna Rabbiyal aʿlā wa biḥamdih

I declare that my Most High Nurturer is free from imperfections, and I do so by praising Him.

Tasbiḥ x 10

سُبْحَانَ اللهِ

Subḥān Allah

I declare that Allah is free from imperfections

وَ الْحَمْدُ لِلّهِ

Walḥamdu lillāh

And all praise is for Allah

وَ لاَ إِلٰهَ إِلاَّ اللهُ

Wa lā ilāha illal lāh

And there is no god but Allah

وَ اللهُ أَكْبَرُ

Wallahu Akbar

And Allah is greater (than what He is described as)

1st *rakʿah*

- After the second *sajdah*, sit up and recite the *tasbiḥs* 10 times
- That's 75 *tasbiḥs* in total

Tasbiḥ x 10

سُبْحَانَ اللهِ

Subḥān Allah

I declare that Allah is free from imperfections

وَ الْحَمْدُ لِلّٰهِ

Walḥamdu lillāh

And all praise is for Allah

وَ لاَ إِلٰهَ إِلاَّ اللهُ

Wa lā ilāha illal lāh

And there is no god but Allah

وَ اللهُ أَكْبَرُ

Wallahu Akbar

And Allah is greater (than what He is described as)

1st *rak'ah*

- Stand up for the second *rak'ah*
- Recite Sūrah al-Fātiḥah
- Now recite Sūrah al-'Ādiyāt once

Sūrah al-Fātiḥah and Sūrah al-'Ādiyāt

2nd *rak'ah*

بِسْمِ اللَّهِ الرَّحْمَٰنِ الرَّحِيمِ

Bismil lāhir Raḥmānir Raḥīm
I start in the name of Allah, The All-Merciful, The Kindest towards believers.

وَالْعَادِيَاتِ ضَبْحًا

Wal 'ādiyāti ḍabḥā
I swear by the charging, panting horses,

فَالْمُورِيَاتِ قَدْحًا

Fal mūriyāti qadḥā
striking sparks of fire (with their hooves).

فَالْمُغِيرَاتِ صُبْحًا

Fal mughīrāti ṣubḥā
charging, ambushing at dawn,

فَأَثَرْنَ بِهِ نَقْعًا

Fa atharna bihi naq'ā
raising clouds of dust,

فَوَسَطْنَ بِهِ جَمْعًا

Fawasaṭna bihi jam'ā
penetrating through the middle (of the enemy).

إِنَّ الْإِنسَانَ لِرَبِّهِ لَكَنُودٌ

Innal insāna lirabbihi lakanūd
Indeed, the human being is extremely ungrateful to his Nurturer.

وَإِنَّهُ عَلَىٰ ذَٰلِكَ لَشَهِيدٌ

Wa innahu 'alā dhālika lashahīd
And he is surely a witness to that.

وَإِنَّهُ لِحُبِّ الْخَيْرِ لَشَدِيدٌ

Wa innahu liḥubbil khayri lashadīd
And indeed, he has intense love for wealth.

أَفَلَا يَعْلَمُ إِذَا بُعْثِرَ مَا فِي الْقُبُورِ

Afalā ya'lamu idhā bu'thira mā fil qubūr
Does he not know that when those in the graves will be raised,

وَحُصِّلَ مَا فِي الصُّدُورِ

Wa ḥuṣṣila mā fiṣ ṣudūr
and whatever is (hidden) in the hearts will become known?

إِنَّ رَبَّهُم بِهِمْ يَوْمَئِذٍ لَخَبِيرٌ

Inna rabbahum bihim yawma idhi(n)l lakhabīr
Indeed, on that day; they will know that their Nurturer (already) had full knowledge of them.

Now recite 15 *tasbiḥs*

Tasbiḥ x 15

سُبْحَانَ اللهِ

Subḥān Allah

I declare that Allah is free from imperfections

وَ الْحَمْدُ لِلّهِ

Walḥamdu lillāh

And all praise is for Allah

وَ لاَ إِلهَ إِلاَّ اللهُ

Wa lā ilāha illal lāh

And there is no god but Allah

وَ اللهُ أَكْبَرُ

Wallahu Akbar

And Allah is greater (than what He is described as)

2nd *rakʿah*

It is recommended to perform *qunūt* and recite all your needs if preferred

2nd *rakʿah*

Repeat the same as the first *rakʿah* by doing *rukūʿ* and the two *sajdahs* with 10 *tasbiḥs* after each movement
10 *tasbiḥs*
10 *tasbiḥs*
10 *tasbiḥs*
10 *tasbiḥs*
10 *tasbiḥs*
10 *tasbiḥs*
2nd *rakʿah*

- That's 150 *tasbiḥs* in total
- After the two *sajdahs* recite the *tashahhud* and then recite *taslīm*

Tashahhud

اشْهَدُ اَنْ لااِلٰهَ اِلاَّ اللهُ وَحْدَهُ لاشَرِيكَ لَهُ

Ashhadu a(n)l lā ilāha illa lāhu waḥdahu lā sharīka lah

I testify that there is no god but Allah, He is alone, for whom there is no partner.

وَ أَشْهَدُ أَنَّ مُحَمَّداً عَبْدُهُ وَ رَسُولُه

Wa ashhadu anna Muḥammadan ʿabduhu wa rasūluh

And I testify that Muḥammad is His servant and His messenger.

أَللّٰهُمَّ صَلِّ عَلىٰ مُحَمَّدٍ وَ آلِ مُحَمَّد

Allahumma ṣalli ʿalā Muḥammadi(n)w wa āli Muḥammad

O Allah! Bless Muḥammad and the progeny of Muḥammad.

Taslīm

اَلسَّلامُ عَلَيْكَ اَيُّها ٱلنَّبِيُّ وَ رَحْمَةُ اللهِ وَ بَرَكاتُه

Assalāmu ʿalayka ayyuhan nabiyyu wa raḥmatullāhi wa barakātuh

Peace be upon you O Prophet, and Allah's mercy and His blessings (be upon you too).

اَلسَّلامُ عَلَينا وَ عَلىٰ عِبادِ اللهِ الصّالِحِينَ

Assalāmu ʿalaynā wa ʿalā ʿibādillāhiṣ ṣaliḥīn

Peace be upon us and upon the righteous servants of Allah.

السَّلامُ عَلَيْكُمْ وَ رَحْمَةُ اللهِ وَ بَرَكاتُه

Assalāmu ʿalaykum wa raḥmatul lāhi wa barakātuh

Peace be upon you all, and Allah's mercy and His blessings (be upon you too).

2nd *rakʿah*

- Now do this prayer one more time in the same manner as before except with different second *Sūrahs*
- In the first *rakʿah* recite Sūrah al-Fātiḥah and Sūrah al-Naṣr once
- In the second *rakʿah* recite Sūrah al-Fātiḥah and Sūrah al-Ikhlāṣ once

- Remain standing
- Recite Sūrah al-Fātiḥah
- Now recite Sūrah al-Naṣr once

Sūrah al-Fātiḥah and Sūrah al-Naṣr

بِسْمِ اللَّـهِ الرَّحْمَـٰنِ الرَّحِيمِ

Bismil lāhir Raḥmānir Raḥīm
I start in the name of Allah, The All-Merciful, The Kindest towards believers.

إِذَا جَاءَ نَصْرُ اللَّهِ وَالْفَتْحُ

Idhā jā-a naṣrul lāhi wal fatḥ
When the help and victory comes from Allah.

وَرَأَيْتَ النَّاسَ يَدْخُلُونَ فِي دِينِ اللَّهِ أَفْوَاجًا

Wara aytan nāsa yadkhulūna fī dīnil lāhi afwājā
And when you see the people entering the Religion of Allah in large crowds.

فَسَبِّحْ بِحَمْدِ رَبِّكَ وَاسْتَغْفِرْهُ ۚ إِنَّهُ كَانَ تَوَّابًا

Fasabbiḥ biḥamdi rabbika wastaghfirhu innahu kāna tawwābā
Then glorify and praise your Nurturer and seek His forgiveness. Indeed, He is the one who accepts repentance.

1st rakʿah

Now recite 15 *tasbiḥs*

Tasbiḥ x 15

سُبْحَانَ اللهِ

Subḥān Allah

I declare that Allah is free from imperfections

وَ الْحَمْدُ لِلّهِ

Walḥamdu lillāh

And all praise is for Allah

وَ لاَ إِلٰهَ إِلاَّ اللهُ

Wa lā ilāha illal lāh

And there is no god but Allah

وَ اللهُ أَكْبَرُ

Wallahu Akbar

And Allah is greater (than what He is described as)

1st *rakʿah*

Perform the *rukūʿ* and the two *sajdahs* with 10 *tasbiḥs* after each movement
10 *tasbiḥs*
10 *tasbiḥs*
10 *tasbiḥs*
10 *tasbiḥs*
10 *tasbiḥs*
10 *tasbiḥs*
1st *rakʿah*

- Stand up for the second *rakʿah*
- Recite Sūrah al-Fātiḥah
- Now recite Sūrah al-Ikhlāṣ once

بِسْمِ اللَّـهِ الرَّحْمَـٰنِ الرَّحِيمِ

Bismil lāhir Raḥmānir Raḥīm

I start in the name of Allah, The All-Merciful, The Kindest towards believers.

قُلْ هُوَ اللَّـهُ أَحَدٌ

Qul huwal lāhu aḥad

Say, He is Allah, the One.

اللَّـهُ الصَّمَدُ

Allahuṣ Ṣamad

Allah is Who is independent of all beings.

لَمْ يَلِدْ وَلَمْ يُولَدْ

Lam yalid wa lam yūlad

He has never had an offspring, nor was He born.

وَلَمْ يَكُن لَّهُ كُفُوًا أَحَدٌ

Wa lam yaku(n)l lahu kufuwan aḥad

Nor has He any equal.

2nd *rakʿah*

Now recite 15 *tasbiḥs*

Tasbiḥ x 15

سُبْحَانَ اللهِ

Subḥān Allah

I declare that Allah is free from imperfections

وَ الْحَمْدُ لِلّٰهِ

Walḥamdu lillāh

And all praise is for Allah

وَ لاَ إِلٰهَ إِلاَّ اللّٰهُ

Wa lā ilāha illal lāh

And there is no god but Allah

وَ اللّٰهُ أَكْبَرُ

Wallahu Akbar

And Allah is greater (than what He is described as)

2nd *rakʿah*

It is recommended to perform *qunūt* and recite all your needs if preferred
2nd *rakʿah*

Repeat the same as the first *rakʿah* by doing *rukūʿ* and the two *sajdahs* with 10 *tasbiḥs* after each movement
10 *tasbiḥs*
10 *tasbiḥs*
10 *tasbiḥs*
10 *tasbiḥs*
2nd *rakʿah*
10 *tasbiḥs*

2nd *sajdah*

- While in the second *sajdah* after the *dhikr* and after the 10 *tasbiḥs*, it is recommended to recite the following supplication ....
- After the supplication it is recommended to mention your needs

سُبْحَانَ مَنْ لَبِسَ ٱلْعِزَّ وَٱلْوَقَارَ

Subḥāna man labisal ʿizza wal waqār

Glory be to Him Who has dressed Himself dignity and sobriety!

سُبْحَانَ مَنْ تَعَطَّفَ بِٱلْمَجْدِ وَتَكَرَّمَ بِهِ

Subḥāna man taʿaṭṭafa bilmajdi wa takarrama bih

Glory be to Him Who has deigned and condescended with grandeur!

سُبْحَانَ مَنْ لاَ يَنْبَغِي ٱلتَّسْبِيحُ إِلاَّ لَهُ

Subḥāna man lā yanbaghit tasbīḥu illā lah

Glory be to Him save Whom none is worthy of being glorified!

سُبْحَانَ مَنْ اَحْصَىٰ كُلَّ شَيْءٍ عِلْمُهُ

Subḥāna man aḥṣā kulla shayin ʿilmuh

Glory be to Him Whose knowledge has counted all things!

سُبْحَانَ ذِي ٱلْمَنِّ وَٱلنِّعَمِ

Subḥāna dhil manni wan niʿam

Glory be to the Nurturer of bounty and boon!

سُبْحَانَ ذِي ٱلْقُدْرَةِ وَٱلْكَرَمِ

Subḥāna dhil qudrati wal karam

Glory be to the Nurturer of omnipotence and nobility!

اَللَّهُمَّ إِنِّي اسْأَلُكَ بِمَعَاقِدِ ٱلْعِزِّ مِنْ عَرْشِكَ

Allahumma inni as aluka bimaʿāqidil ʿizzi min ʿarshik

O Allah, I beseech You in the name of the objects of dignity in Your Throne,

وَمُنْتَهَىٰ ٱلرَّحْمَةِ مِنْ كِتَابِكَ

Wa muntahar raḥmati min kitābik

and in the name of the utmost of mercy in Your Book,

وَٱسْمِكَ ٱلاعْظَمِ وَكَلِمَاتِكَ ٱلتَّامَّةِ ٱلَّتِي تَمَّتْ صِدْقاً وَعَدْلاً

Wasmikal aʿẓami wa kalimātikat tāmmah, allatī tammat ṣidqa(n)w wa ʿadlā

and in the name of Your Greatest Name, and Your Accomplished Words, which have been accomplished truly and justly.

صَلِّ عَلَىٰ مُحَمَّدٍ وَاهْلِ بَيْتِهِ.......

Ṣalli ʿalā muḥammadi(n)w wa ahli baytih.....

(Please) send blessings to Muḥammad and his Household.... **(mention needs)**

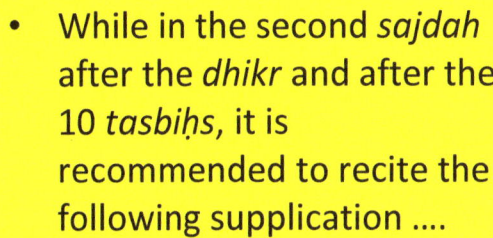

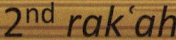

2nd *rakʿah*

- After the second *sajdah*, sit up and recite the *tasbiḥs* 10 times
- That's 300 *tasbiḥs* in total for both prayers

Tasbiḥ x 10

سُبْحَانَ اللهِ

Subḥān Allah

I declare that Allah is free from imperfections

وَ الْحَمْدُ لِلهِ

Walḥamdu lillāh

And all praise is for Allah

وَ لاَ إِلهَ إِلاَّ اللهُ

Wa lā ilāha illal lāh

And there is no god but Allah

وَ اللهُ أَكْبَرُ

Wallahu Akbar

And Allah is greater (than what He is described as)

2nd *rakʿah*

Recite the *tashahhud* and then recite *taslīm*

Tashahhud

اشْهَدُ اَنْ لااِلٰهَ اِلاَّ اللهُ وَحْدَهُ لاشَرِيكَ لَهُ

Ashhadu a(n)l lā ilāha illa lāhu waḥdahu lā sharīka lah

I testify that there is no god but Allah, He is alone, for whom there is no partner.

وَ أَشْهَدُ أَنَّ مُحَمَّداً عَبْدُهُ وَ رَسُولُه

Wa ashhadu anna Muḥammadan ʿabduhu wa rasūluh

And I testify that Muḥammad is His servant and His messenger.

أَللّٰهُمَّ صَلِّ عَلىٰ مُحَمَّدٍ وَ آلِ مُحَمَّد

Allahumma ṣalli ʿalā Muḥammadi(n)w wa āli Muḥammad

O Allah! Bless Muḥammad and the progeny of Muḥammad.

Taslīm

اَلسَّلامُ عَلَيْكَ اَيُّها ٱلنَّبِيُّ وَ رَحْمَةُ اللهِ وَ بَرَكاتُه

Assalāmu ʿalayka ayyuhan nabiyyu wa raḥmatullāhi wa barakātuh

Peace be upon you O Prophet, and Allah's mercy and His blessings (be upon you too).

اَلسَّلامُ عَلَينا وَ عَلىٰ عِبادِ اللهِ الصّالِحِينَ

Assalāmu ʿalaynā wa ʿalā ʿibādillāhiṣ ṣaliḥīn

Peace be upon us and upon the righteous servants of Allah.

السَّلامُ عَلَيْكُمْ وَ رَحْمَةُ اللهِ وَ بَرَكاتُه

Assalāmu ʿalaykum wa raḥmatul lāhi wa barakātuh

Peace be upon you all, and Allah's mercy and His blessings (be upon you too).

2nd *rakʿah*

After performing the prayer, it is also recommended to raise your hands and recite each of the supplications as many times as possible until one is out of breath

One Breath Each

يَا رَبِّ يَا رَبِّ

Yā rabbi yā rabbi ......

O Nurturer, O Nurturer.....

يَا رَبَّاهُ يَا رَبَّاهُ

Yā rabbāhu yā rabbāhu ......

O my Nurturer, O my Nurturer.....

رَبِّ رَبِّ

Rabbi rabbi ......

Nurturer, Nurturer.....

يَا اللّٰهُ يَا اللّٰهُ

Yā Allahu yā Allahu ......

O Allah, O Allah.....

يَا حَيُّ يَا حَيُّ

Yā ḥayyu ya ḥayyu ......

O Ever-living, O Ever-living.....

يَا رَحِيمُ يَا رَحِيمُ

Yā raḥīmu ya raḥīmu ......

O All-Merciful, O All-Merciful.....

Now repeat each sentence 7 times

يَا رَحْمٰنُ يَا رَحْمٰنُ

Yā raḥmānu yā raḥmān x 7

O All-compassionate, O All-compassionate!

يَا أَرْحَمَ الرَّاحِمِينَ

Yā arḥamar rāḥimīn x 7

O Most Merciful of all those who show mercy!

Now it is recommended to recite this supplication

اَللَّهُمَّ اِنِّي اَفْتَتِحُ الْقَوْلَ بِحَمْدِكَ

Allahumma innī aftatiḥul qawla biḥamdik

O Allah, I commence my wording with declaring praise to You,

وَ اَنْطِقُ بِالثَّنَاءِ عَلَيْكَ

Wa anṭiqu bith thanā-i ʿalayk

and I utter the words of tribute to You,

وَ اُمَجِّدُكَ وَ لا غَايَةَ لِمَدْحِكَ

Wa umajjiduka wa lā ghāyata limad ḥik

and I glorify You although Your glory is limitless,

وَ اُثْنِي عَلَيْكَ وَ مَنْ يَبْلُغُ غَايَةَ ثَنَائِكَ وَ اَمَدَ مَجْدِكَ

Wa uthnī ʿalayka wa man yablughu ghāyata thanā ika wa amada majdik

and I compliment You although none can ever compliment You as much as You deserve, and none can ever attain the extent of Your glory!

وَ اَنَّى لِخَلِيقَتِكَ كُنْهُ مَعْرِفَةِ مَجْدِكَ

Wa annā likhalīqatika kunhu maʿrifati majdik

And how can Your creatures ever recognize Your Glory.

وَ اَيَّ زَمَنٍ لَمْ تَكُنْ مَمْدُوحاً بِفَضْلِكَ

Wa ayya zamanin lam takun mamdūḥan bifaḍlik

And how can there be any moment for which You do not deserve praise due to Your favours,

مَوْصُوفاً بِمَجْدِكَ عَوَّاداً عَلَى الْمُذْنِبِينَ بِحِلْمِكَ

Mawṣūfan bimajdik, ʿawwādan ʿalal mudhnibīna biḥilmik

in which You are not ascribed to glory and in which You do not incessantly treat the sinful with Your forbearance?

تَخَلَّفَ سُكَّانُ اَرْضِكَ عَنْ طَاعَتِكَ

Takhallafa sukkānu arḍika ʿan ṭāʿatik

Although the inhabitants of Your earth have fallen behind in being obedient to You,

فَكُنْتَ عَلَيْهِمْ عَطُوفاً بِجُودِكَ

Fakunta ʿalayhim ʿaṭūfan bijūdik

You have been kind to them out of Your munificence,

جَوَاداً بِفَضْلِكَ عَوَّاداً بِكَرَمِكَ

Jawādan bifaḍlik, ʿawwādan bikaramik

munificent out of Your favours and liberal out of Your generosity.

يَا لا اِلَهَ اِلَّا اَنْتَ الْمَنَّانُ ذُو الْجَلالِ وَ الْاِكْرَامِ

Yā lā ilāha illā antal mannānu dhul jalāli wal ikrām

O He save Whom there is no god! O All-benevolent! O Lord of Glory and Honour!

How to Pray

Ṣalāt al – Eid

2 x *rakʿahs*

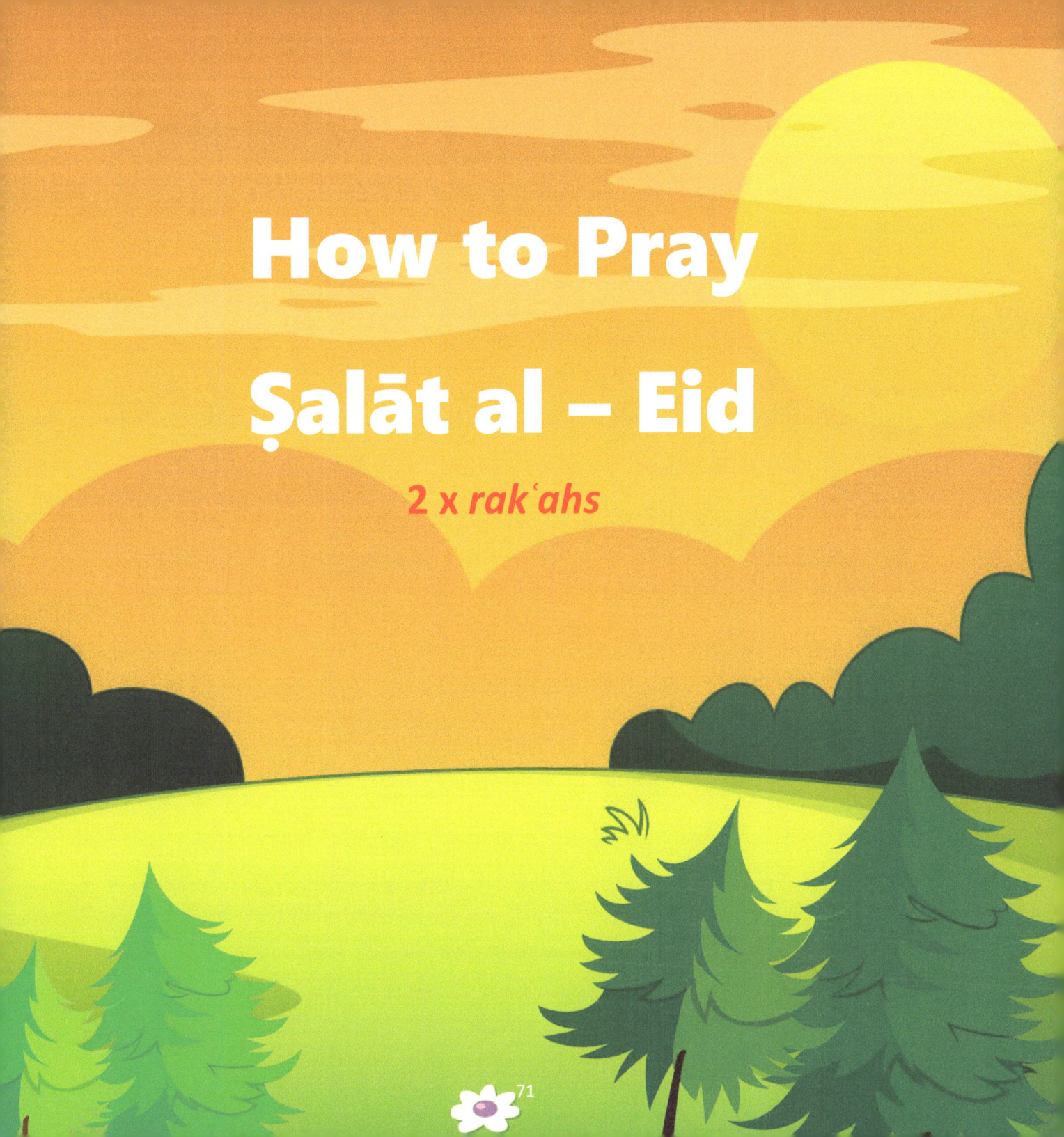

The *Eid al-Fiṭr* and *Eid al-Aḍḥā* prayer is obligatory during the presence of Imām al-Mahdī (as) and must be performed in congregation.

In our time, when the Imām (as) is in occultation, the prayer is recommended, and it can be performed in congregation or alone.

The time for the prayer is from sunrise to the time of *Ẓuhr* prayers on the day of *Eid*.

On the day of *Eid al-Fiṭr* it is recommended after sunrise that you eat something and pay your *Zakāt al-Fiṭrah* first and then perform the prayer.

On *Eid al-Aḍḥā* it is recommended to perform the prayer after sunrise.

It is also recommended to pray in an open field. However, in Mecca, it is recommended to pray in *Masjid al-Ḥarām*.

The prayer consists of 2 *rakʿahs* and in the first *rakʿah* we recite 5 *takbīrs* with 5 *qunūts* and in the second *rakʿah* 4 *takbīrs* and 4 *qunūts*. Some have said 4 *takbīrs* and 4 *qunūts* will be sufficient in both *rakʿahs*.

During the period of occultation of the Imām (as), if the *Eid al-Fiṭr* and *Eid al-Aḍḥā* prayer is performed in congregation, the obligatory precaution is that two sermons must be delivered after the prayer, and the Imām must briefly sit down between the two sermons.

The *Eid* prayer does not have a specified *Sūrah*, but it is better that in the first *rakʿah* Sūrat al-Shams be recited, and in the second *rakʿah* Sūrat al-Ghāshiyah be recited; or, in the first *rakʿah* Sūrat al-Aʿlā be recited, and in the second *rakʿah* Sūrat al-Shams be recited.

- Make your intention
- Perform *Takbīrat al-iḥrām*

- Remain standing
- Recite Sūrah al-Fātiḥah
- Now recite Sūrah al-Aʿlā*

Bismil lāhir Raḥmānir Raḥīm	بِسْمِ اللَّهِ الرَّحْمَٰنِ الرَّحِيمِ
Sabbiḥisma rabbikal aʿlā	سَبِّحِ ٱسْمَ رَبِّكَ ٱلْأَعْلَى
Alladhī khalaqa fasawwā	ٱلَّذِى خَلَقَ فَسَوَّىٰ
Walladhī qaddara fahadā	وَٱلَّذِى قَدَّرَ فَهَدَىٰ
Walladhī akhrajal marʿā	وَٱلَّذِىٓ أَخْرَجَ ٱلْمَرْعَىٰ
Fajaʿalahū ghuthā-an aḥwā	فَجَعَلَهُۥ غُثَآءً أَحْوَىٰ
Sanuqri uka falā tansā	سَنُقْرِئُكَ فَلَا تَنسَىٰٓ
Illā mā shā Allah, innahū yaʿlamul jahra wamā yakhfā	إِلَّا مَا شَآءَ ٱللَّهُ ۚ إِنَّهُۥ يَعْلَمُ ٱلْجَهْرَ وَمَا يَخْفَىٰ
Wanu yassiruka lil yusrā	وَنُيَسِّرُكَ لِلْيُسْرَىٰ
Fadhakkir innafa ʿatidh-dhikrā	فَذَكِّرْ إِن نَّفَعَتِ ٱلذِّكْرَىٰ
Sayadh-dhakkaru ma(n)y yakhshā	سَيَذَّكَّرُ مَن يَخْشَىٰ
Wayatajannabuhal ashqā	وَيَتَجَنَّبُهَا ٱلْأَشْقَى
Alladhī yaṣlan nāral kubrā	ٱلَّذِى يَصْلَى ٱلنَّارَ ٱلْكُبْرَىٰ
Thumma lā yamūtu fīhā walā yaḥyā	ثُمَّ لَا يَمُوتُ فِيهَا وَلَا يَحْيَىٰ
Qad aflaḥa man tazakkā	قَدْ أَفْلَحَ مَن تَزَكَّىٰ
Wa dhakarasma rabbihī faṣallā	وَذَكَرَ ٱسْمَ رَبِّهِۦ فَصَلَّىٰ
Bal tuʾthirūnal ḥayātad dunyā	بَلْ تُؤْثِرُونَ ٱلْحَيَوٰةَ ٱلدُّنْيَا
Wal-ākhiratu khayru(n)w wa abqā	وَٱلْءَاخِرَةُ خَيْرٌ وَأَبْقَىٰٓ
Inna hādhā lafiṣ ṣuḥufil ūlā	إِنَّ هَٰذَا لَفِى ٱلصُّحُفِ ٱلْأُولَىٰ
Ṣuḥufi ibrāhīma wa mūsā	صُحُفِ إِبْرَٰهِيمَ وَمُوسَىٰ

*translation on pg. 80

1st *rakʿah*

- Perform *takbīr* (Allahu Akbar)
- Perform *qunūt* with the recommended *dua**
- After the *dua,* perform *takbīr* again
- Do this method 5 times all up
- That would be a total of 5 *qunūts* and 5 *takbīrs*

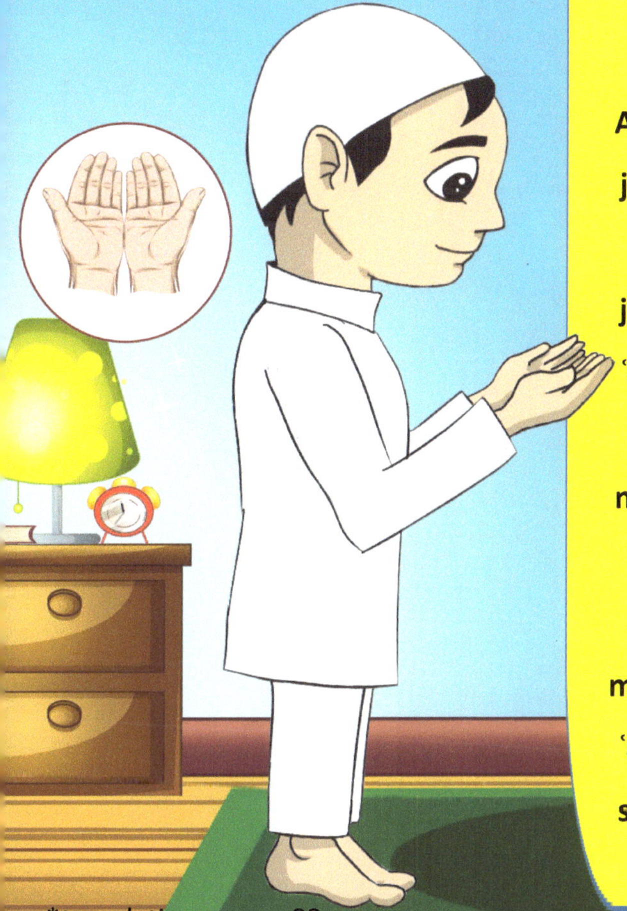

X 5

اَللّٰهُمَّ أَهْلَ الْكِبْرِيَاءِ وَالْعَظَمَةِ، وَأَهْلَ الْجُوْدِ وَالْجَبَرُوْتِ، وَأَهْلَ الْعَفْوِ
وَالرَّحْمَةِ، وَأَهْلَ التَّقْوٰى وَالْمَغْفِرَةِ، أَسْأَلُكَ بِحَقِّ هٰذَا الْيَوْمِ، اَلَّذِيْ
جَعَلْتَهُ لِلْمُسْلِمِيْنَ عِيْدًا، وَلِمُحَمَّدٍ صَلَّى اللهُ عَلَيْهِ وَآلِهِ وَسَلَّمَ، ذُخْرًا
وَشَرَفًا وَكَرَامَةً وَمَزِيْدًا، أَنْ تُصَلِّيَ عَلٰى مُحَمَّدٍ وَآلِ مُحَمَّدٍ، وَأَنْ
تُدْخِلَنِيْ فِي كُلِّ خَيْرٍ أَدْخَلْتَ فِيْهِ مُحَمَّدًا وَآلَ مُحَمَّدٍ، وَأَنْ تُخْرِجَنِيْ
مِنْ كُلِّ سُوْءٍ أَخْرَجْتَ مِنْهُ مُحَمَّدًا وَآلَ مُحَمَّدٍ صَلَوَاتُكَ عَلَيْهِ وَعَلَيْهِمْ،
اَللّٰهُمَّ إِنِّي أَسْأَلُكَ خَيْرَ مَا سَأَلَكَ بِهِ عِبَادُكَ الصَّالِحُوْنَ، وَأَعُوْذُ بِكَ مِمَّا
اَسْتَعَاذَ مِنْهُ عِبَادُكَ الْمُخْلَصُوْنَ

Allāhumma ahlal kibriyā i wal ʿaẓamah, wa ahlal jūdi wal jabarūt, wa ahlal ʿafwi war raḥmah, wa ahlat taqwā wal maghfirah, as aluka biḥaqqi hādhal yawm, alladhī jaʿaltahu lilmuslimīna ʿīdā, wa limuḥammadin ṣallallāhu ʿalayhi wa ālihi wa sallam, dhukhra(n)w wa sharafa(n)w wa karāmata(n)w wa mazīdā, an tuṣalliya ʿalā muḥammadi(n)w wa āli muḥammad, wa an tudkhilanī fī kulli khayrin adkhalta fīhi muḥammada(n)w wa āla muḥammad, wa an tukhrijanī min kulli sū in akhrajta minhu muḥammada(n)w wa āla muḥammad, ṣalawātuka ʿalayhi wa ʿalayhim, allāhumma innī as aluka khayra mā sa alaka bihi ʿibādukaṣ ṣāliḥūn, wa aʿūdhu bika mimmas taʿādha minhu ʿibādukal mukhlaṣūn

*translation on pg. 82

Perform the *rukūʿ* and the two *sajdahs*
1
2
3
4
5
6
1st *rakʿah*

- Stand back up for the second *rakʿah*
- Recite Sūrah al-Fātiḥah
- Now recite Sūrah al-Shams*

Bismil lāhir Raḥmānir Raḥīm	بِسْمِ اللَّـهِ الرَّحْمَـٰنِ الرَّحِيمِ
Wash-shamsi waḍuḥāhā	وَٱلشَّمْسِ وَضُحَىٰهَا
Wal qamari idhā talāhā	وَٱلْقَمَرِ إِذَا تَلَىٰهَا
Wan nahāri idhā jallāhā	وَٱلنَّهَارِ إِذَا جَلَّىٰهَا
Wal layli idhā yaghshāhā	وَٱلَّيْلِ إِذَا يَغْشَىٰهَا
Was samā-i wamā banāhā	وَٱلسَّمَآءِ وَمَا بَنَىٰهَا
Wal arḍi wamā ṭaḥāhā	وَٱلْأَرْضِ وَمَا طَحَىٰهَا
Wanafsi(n)w wamā sawwāhā	وَنَفْسٍ وَمَا سَوَّىٰهَا
Fa alhamahā fujūrahā wataqwāhā	فَأَلْهَمَهَا فُجُورَهَا وَتَقْوَىٰهَا
Qad aflaḥa man zakkāhā	قَدْ أَفْلَحَ مَن زَكَّىٰهَا
Waqad khāba man dassāhā	وَقَدْ خَابَ مَن دَسَّىٰهَا
Kadh dhabat thamūdu biṭaghwāhā	كَذَّبَتْ ثَمُودُ بِطَغْوَىٰهَآ
Idhim baʿatha ashqāhā	إِذِ ٱنۢبَعَثَ أَشْقَىٰهَا
Fa qāla lahum rasūlul lāhi nāqatal lāhi wasuq yāhā	فَقَالَ لَهُمْ رَسُولُ ٱللَّهِ نَاقَةَ ٱللَّهِ وَسُقْيَـٰهَا
Fakadh dhabūhu faʿaqarūhā fadamdama ʿalayhim rabbuhum bidhambihim fasawwāhā	فَكَذَّبُوهُ فَعَقَرُوهَا فَدَمْدَمَ عَلَيْهِمْ رَبُّهُم بِذَنۢبِهِمْ فَسَوَّىٰهَا
Walā yakhāfu ʿuqbāhā	وَلَا يَخَافُ عُقْبَـٰهَا

*translation on pg. 81

2nd *rakʿah*

- Perform *takbīr* (Allahu Akbar)
- Perform *qunūt* with the recommended *dua*
- After the *dua* perform *takbīr* again
- Do this method 4 times all up
- That would be a total of 4 *qunūts* and 4 *takbīrs*

X 4

اَللّٰهُمَّ أَهْلَ الْكِبْرِيَاءِ وَالْعَظَمَةِ، وَأَهْلَ الْجُوْدِ وَالْجَبَرُوْتِ، وَأَهْلَ الْعَفْوِ
وَالرَّحْمَةِ، وَأَهْلَ التَّقْوٰى وَالْمَغْفِرَةِ، أَسْأَلُكَ بِحَقِّ هٰذَا الْيَوْمِ، اَلَّذِيْ
جَعَلْتَهُ لِلْمُسْلِمِيْنَ عِيْدًا، وَلِمُحَمَّدٍ صَلَّى اللهُ عَلَيْهِ وَآلِهِ وَسَلَّمَ، ذُخْرًا
وَشَرَفًا وَكَرَامَةً وَمَزِيْدًا، أَنْ تُصَلِّيَ عَلٰى مُحَمَّدٍ وَآلِ مُحَمَّدٍ، وَأَنْ
تُدْخِلَنِيْ فِي كُلِّ خَيْرٍ أَدْخَلْتَ فِيْهِ مُحَمَّدًا وَآلَ مُحَمَّدٍ، وَأَنْ تُخْرِجَنِيْ
مِنْ كُلِّ سُوْءٍ أَخْرَجْتَ مِنْهُ مُحَمَّدًا وَآلَ مُحَمَّدٍ صَلَوَاتُكَ عَلَيْهِ وَعَلَيْهِمْ،
اَللّٰهُمَّ إِنِّي أَسْأَلُكَ خَيْرَ مَا سَأَلَكَ بِهِ عِبَادُكَ الصَّالِحُوْنَ، وَأَعُوْذُ بِكَ مِمَّا
اسْتَعَاذَ مِنْهُ عِبَادُكَ الْمُخْلَصُوْنَ

Allāhumma ahlal kibriyā i wal ʿaẓamah, wa ahlal jūdi wal jabarūt, wa ahlal ʿafwi war raḥmah, wa ahlat taqwā wal maghfirah, as aluka biḥaqqi hādhal yawm, alladhī jaʿaltahu lilmuslimīna ʿīdā, wa limuḥammadin ṣallallāhu ʿalayhi wa ālihi wa sallam, dhukhra(n)w wa sharafa(n)w wa karāmata(n)w wa mazīdā, an tuṣalliya ʿalā muḥammadi(n)w wa āli muḥammad, wa an tudkhilanī fī kulli khayrin adkhalta fīhi muḥammada(n)w wa āla muḥammad, wa an tukhrijanī min kulli sū in akhrajta minhu muḥammada(n)w wa āla muḥammad, ṣalawātuka ʿalayhi wa ʿalayhim, allāhumma innī as aluka khayra mā sa alaka bihi ʿibādukaṣ ṣāliḥūn, wa aʿūdhu bika mimmas taʿādha minhu ʿibādukal mukhlaṣūn

2nd *rakʿah*

- Perform the *rukūʿ* and the two *sajdahs*
- Finish the prayer as usual, with *tashahhud* and *taslīm*

Translations

Sūrah al-Aʿlā

I start in the name of Allah, the All Merciful towards all existents, The Kindest towards believers.	بِسْمِ اللَّـهِ الرَّحْمَـٰنِ الرَّحِيمِ
1. Praise the Name of your Nurturer, the Most-High.	سَبِّحِ ٱسْمَ رَبِّكَ ٱلْأَعْلَى
2. Who created and proportioned.	ٱلَّذِى خَلَقَ فَسَوَّىٰ
3. He who measures and guides.	وَٱلَّذِى قَدَّرَ فَهَدَىٰ
4. He who produces the pasture.	وَٱلَّذِىٓ أَخْرَجَ ٱلْمَرْعَىٰ
5. And then turns it into light debris.	فَجَعَلَهُۥ غُثَآءً أَحْوَىٰ
6. We will make you read, and you will not forget.	سَنُقْرِئُكَ فَلَا تَنسَىٰٓ
7. Except what Allah wills. He knows what is declared and what is hidden.	إِلَّا مَا شَآءَ ٱللَّهُ ۚ إِنَّهُۥ يَعْلَمُ ٱلْجَهْرَ وَمَا يَخْفَىٰ
8. We will ease you into the Easy Way.	وَنُيَسِّرُكَ لِلْيُسْرَىٰ
9. So remind, if reminding helps.	فَذَكِّرْ إِن نَّفَعَتِ ٱلذِّكْرَىٰ
10. He who fears (Allah) will be reminded.	سَيَذَّكَّرُ مَن يَخْشَىٰ
11. But the wretched will avoid it.	وَيَتَجَنَّبُهَا ٱلْأَشْقَى
12. He who will burn in the greatest Fire.	ٱلَّذِى يَصْلَى ٱلنَّارَ ٱلْكُبْرَىٰ
13. Where he will neither die, nor live.	ثُمَّ لَا يَمُوتُ فِيهَا وَلَا يَحْيَىٰ
14. Successful is he who purifies himself.	قَدْ أَفْلَحَ مَن تَزَكَّىٰ
15. And mentions the name of his Nurturer and prays.	وَذَكَرَ ٱسْمَ رَبِّهِۦ فَصَلَّىٰ
16. But you prefer the present life.	بَلْ تُؤْثِرُونَ ٱلْحَيَوٰةَ ٱلدُّنْيَا
17. Though the Hereafter is better, and ever lasting.	وَٱلْـَٔاخِرَةُ خَيْرٌ وَأَبْقَىٰٓ
18. Indeed, this is in the former scriptures.	إِنَّ هَـٰذَا لَفِى ٱلصُّحُفِ ٱلْأُولَىٰ
19. The Scriptures of Abraham and Moses.	صُحُفِ إِبْرَٰهِيمَ وَمُوسَىٰ

Translations

Sūrah al-Shams

I start in the name of Allah, the All Merciful towards all existents,
The Kindest towards believers.

1. By the sun and its radiance.
2. And the moon as it follows it.
3. And the day as it reveals it.
4. And the night as it conceals it.
5. And the sky and He who built it.
6. And the earth and He who spread it.
7. And the soul and He who proportioned it.
8. And inspired it to understand what was right and wrong for it.
9. Successful is he who purifies it.
10. And he has failed who instills it [with corruption].
11. The Thamud tribe rejected the truth because of their arrogance,
12. When the most wicked man among them rose up.
13. The Messenger of Allah said to them,
    "This is the she-camel of Allah, so let her drink."
14. But they called him a liar and hamstrung her.
    So their Nurturer crushed them for their
    sin and leveled it.
15. And He does not fear the consequence thereof.

بِسْمِ اللَّـهِ الرَّحْمَـٰنِ الرَّحِيمِ

وَٱلشَّمْسِ وَضُحَىٰهَا
وَٱلْقَمَرِ إِذَا تَلَىٰهَا
وَٱلنَّهَارِ إِذَا جَلَّىٰهَا
وَٱلَّيْلِ إِذَا يَغْشَىٰهَا
وَٱلسَّمَآءِ وَمَا بَنَىٰهَا
وَٱلْأَرْضِ وَمَا طَحَىٰهَا
وَنَفْسٍ وَمَا سَوَّىٰهَا
فَأَلْهَمَهَا فُجُورَهَا وَتَقْوَىٰهَا
قَدْ أَفْلَحَ مَن زَكَّىٰهَا
وَقَدْ خَابَ مَن دَسَّىٰهَا
كَذَّبَتْ ثَمُودُ بِطَغْوَىٰهَآ
إِذِ ٱنۢبَعَثَ أَشْقَىٰهَا
فَقَالَ لَهُمْ رَسُولُ ٱللَّهِ نَاقَةَ ٱللَّهِ وَسُقْيَـٰهَا
فَكَذَّبُوهُ فَعَقَرُوهَا فَدَمْدَمَ عَلَيْهِمْ رَبُّهُم بِذَنۢبِهِمْ فَسَوَّىٰهَا
وَلَا يَخَافُ عُقْبَـٰهَا

Translations

Dua for *Qunūt*

اَللّٰهُمَّ أَهْلَ الْكِبْرِيَاءِ وَالْعَظَمَةِ، وَأَهْلَ الْجُوْدِ وَالْجَبَرُوْتِ، وَأَهْلَ الْعَفْوِ وَالرَّحْمَةِ، وَأَهْلَ التَّقْوٰى وَالْمَغْفِرَةِ، أَسْأَلُكَ بِحَقِّ
هٰذَا الْيَوْمِ، اَلَّذِيْ جَعَلْتَهُ لِلْمُسْلِمِيْنَ عِيْدًا، وَلِمُحَمَّدٍ صَلَّى اللهُ عَلَيْهِ وَآلِهِ وَسَلَّمَ، ذُخْرًا وَشَرَفًا وَكَرَامَةً وَمَزِيْدًا، أَنْ تُصَلِّيَ
عَلٰى مُحَمَّدٍ وَآلِ مُحَمَّدٍ، وَأَنْ تُدْخِلَنِيْ فِيْ كُلِّ خَيْرٍ أَدْخَلْتَ فِيْهِ مُحَمَّدًا وَآلَ مُحَمَّدٍ، وَأَنْ تُخْرِجَنِيْ مِنْ كُلِّ سُوْءٍ أَخْرَجْتَ
مِنْهُ مُحَمَّدًا وَآلَ مُحَمَّدٍ صَلَوَاتُكَ عَلَيْهِ وَعَلَيْهِمْ، اَللّٰهُمَّ إِنِّيْ أَسْأَلُكَ خَيْرَ مَا سَأَلَكَ بِهِ عِبَادُكَ الصَّالِحُوْنَ، وَأَعُوْذُ بِكَ مِمَّا
اسْتَعَاذَ مِنْهُ عِبَادُكَ الْمُخْلَصُوْنَ

O Allah! Worthy of supremacy and greatness, and worthy of magnanimity and omnipotence, and worthy of pardoning and showing mercy, and worthy of being wary of and forgiving: I beseech You by the right of this day – which You have appointed to be an Eid for the Muslims, and to be for Muḥammad, may Allah shower His blessings upon, and extend His salutations to, him and his progeny, [a source for] accumulating [Your blessings], and [a source of] honour, nobility, and increase [in Your blessings] – that You bless Muḥammad and the progeny of Muḥammad, and that You place me in every goodness in which You placed Muḥammad and the progeny of Muḥammad, and that You remove me from every evil from which You removed Muḥammad and the progeny of Muḥammad, may Your blessings be upon him and upon them. O Allah! I indeed beseech You for the good for which Your righteous servants have beseeched You, and I seek protection in You from all that for which Your purified servants have sought Your protection.

How to Pray Ṣalāt al – Waḥshah

2 x *rakʿahs*

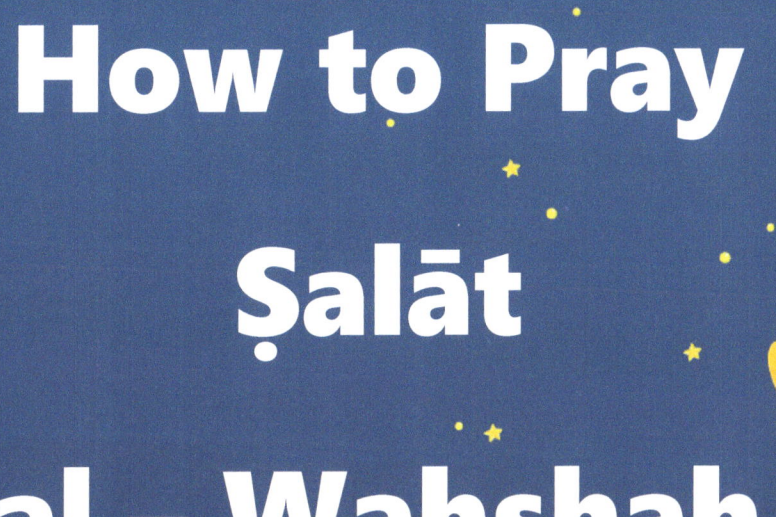

Ṣalāt al-Waḥshah (the prayer of loneliness), is a prayer that is recited on the first night that a Muslim has been buried. It is called *Ṣalāt al-Waḥshah* because on that night, the person buried feels fear and terror as a result of not being familiar with his new home and the conditions that he faces. This prayer, by the mercy of Allah, will remove this fear from the newly deceased person.

The Holy Prophet (saw) is reported to have said:

"**No time passes on the deceased more difficult than the first night in the grave. So have pity on your dead ones and give charity on their behalf and if you cannot, perform two *rak'ahs* of prayer for them**." (*Mafātīḥ al Jinān*)

As you can see from this narration, it is very important to give charity on behalf of the dead person first. And if that is not possible, it is recommended to pray a 2 *rak'ah* prayer.

The prayer must be performed at the first night after burial, so if the burial is postponed, performing the prayer should be postponed as well.

The prayer can be performed anytime on the first night after burial, but it is better to be performed at the early part of the night, after *'Ishā'* prayer.

It is narrated in traditions that this prayer will cause ease for the deceased person and will also cause a widening of their grave. The person who recites this prayer will have many rewards given to them and will be raised 40 ranks by the will of Allah.

The prayer consists of 2 *rak'ahs* and there are two methods of this prayer, but we will demonstrate the most famous method.

- Make your intention
- Perform *Takbīrat al-iḥrām*

- Recite Sūrah al-Fātiḥah
- Now recite al-Kursī verses (2:255 to 257)*

Al-Kursī verses

اَللَّـهُ لَا إِلَـٰهَ إِلَّا هُوَ الْحَيُّ الْقَيُّومُ لَا تَأْخُذُهُ سِنَةٌ وَلَا نَوْمٌ لَّهُ مَا فِي السَّمَاوَاتِ
وَمَا فِي الْأَرْضِ مَن ذَا الَّذِي يَشْفَعُ عِندَهُ إِلَّا بِإِذْنِهِ يَعْلَمُ مَا بَيْنَ أَيْدِيهِمْ وَمَا
خَلْفَهُمْ وَلَا يُحِيطُونَ بِشَيْءٍ مِّنْ عِلْمِهِ إِلَّا بِمَا شَاءَ وَسِعَ كُرْسِيُّهُ السَّمَاوَاتِ
وَالْأَرْضَ وَلَا يَئُودُهُ حِفْظُهُمَا وَهُوَ الْعَلِيُّ الْعَظِيمُ (٢٥٥)

Allahu lā ilāha illā huwal ḥayul qayūm lā ta᾿khudhuhu sinatu(n)w walā nawm, lahu mā fīs samāwāti wamā fil arḍ, man dhal ladhī yashfa῾u ῾indahu illā bi idhnih, ya῾lamu mā bayna aydīhim wamā khalfahum, walā yuḥīṭūna bishayim min ῾ilmihi illā bimā shā᾿, wasi῾a kursiyyuhus samāwāti wal arḍ, walā yaūduhu ḥif ẓuhumā, wahuwal ῾aliyul ῾aẓīm.

لَا إِكْرَاهَ فِي الدِّينِ قَد تَّبَيَّنَ الرُّشْدُ مِنَ الْغَيِّ فَمَن يَكْفُرْ بِالطَّاغُوتِ وَيُؤْمِن
بِاللَّـهِ فَقَدِ اسْتَمْسَكَ بِالْعُرْوَةِ الْوُثْقَىٰ لَا انفِصَامَ لَهَا وَاللَّـهُ سَمِيعٌ عَلِيمٌ (٢٥٦)

Lā ikrāha fid dīn, qat tabayyanar rushdu minal ghay, famay yakfur biṭ ṭāghūti wayu᾿min billāhi faqadis tamsaka bil ῾urwatil wuthqā lanfiṣāma lahā, wallāhu samī῾un ῾alīm.

اللَّـهُ وَلِيُّ الَّذِينَ آمَنُوا يُخْرِجُهُم مِّنَ الظُّلُمَاتِ إِلَى النُّورِ وَالَّذِينَ كَفَرُوا
أَوْلِيَاؤُهُمُ الطَّاغُوتُ يُخْرِجُونَهُم مِّنَ النُّورِ إِلَى الظُّلُمَاتِ أُولَـٰئِكَ أَصْحَابُ النَّارِ
هُمْ فِيهَا خَالِدُونَ (٢٥٧)

Allahu waliyyul ladhīna āmanū yukhrijuhum minaẓ ẓulumāti ilan nūr, wal ladhīna kafarū awliyā uhumuṭ-ṭāghūtu yukhrijūnahum minan nūri ilāẓ-ẓulumāt, ulāika aṣḥābun nār, hum fīhā khālidūn

*translation on pg. 91

1st *rak῾ah*

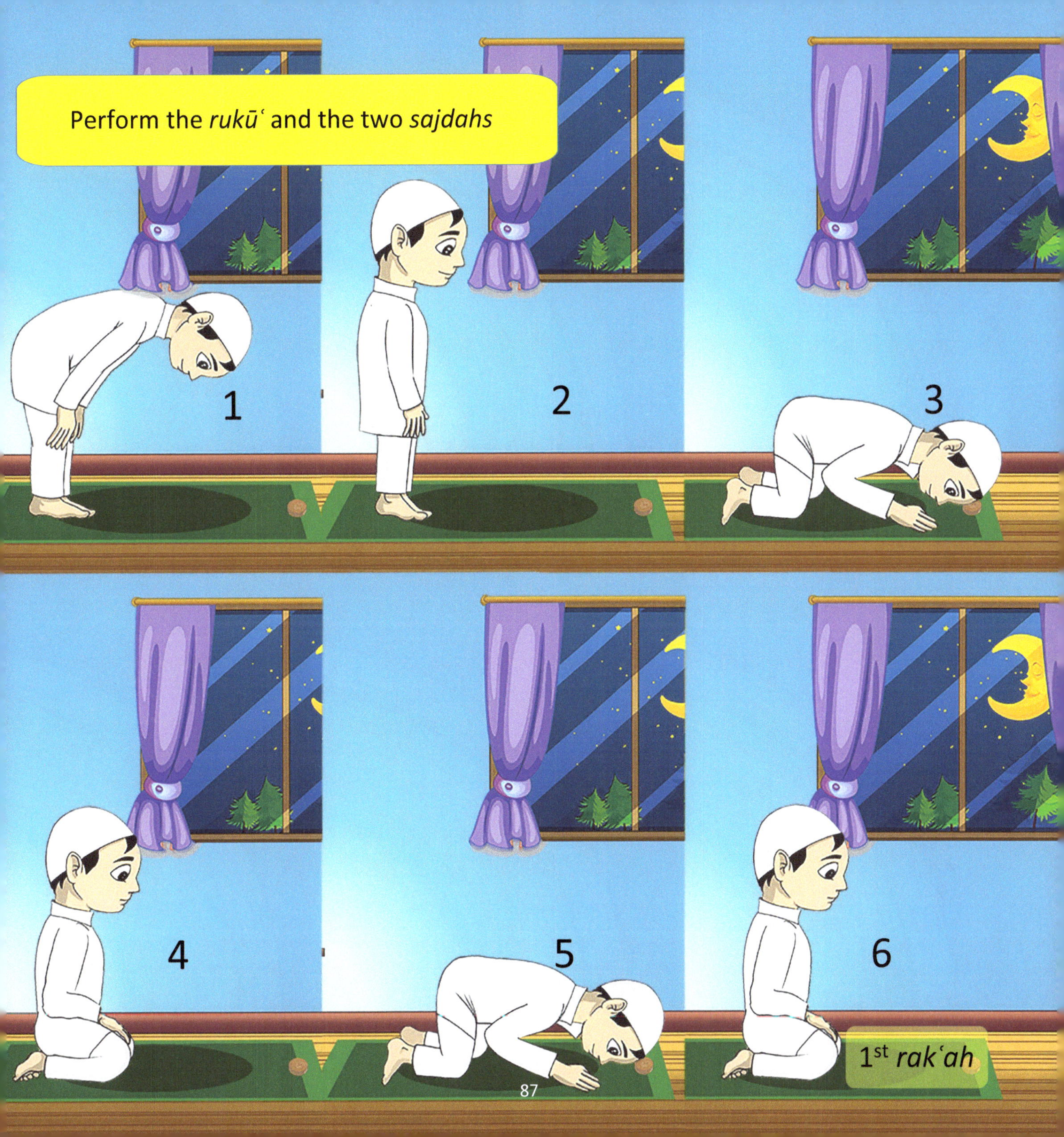
Perform the *rukūʿ* and the two *sajdahs*
1
2
3
4
5
6
1st *rakʿah*

- Stand back up for the second *rakʿah*
- Recite Sūrah al-Fātiḥah
- Now recite Sūrah al-Qadr 10 times

Sūrah al-Qadr x 10

بِسْمِ اللَّـهِ الرَّحْمَـٰنِ الرَّحِيمِ

Bismil lāhir Raḥmānir Raḥīm

I start in the name of Allah, The All-Merciful, The Kindest towards believers.

إِنَّا أَنزَلْنَاهُ فِي لَيْلَةِ الْقَدْرِ

Innā anzalnāhu fī laylatil qadr

Indeed, We revealed it in (the) Night (of) Power.

وَمَا أَدْرَاكَ مَا لَيْلَةُ الْقَدْرِ

wamā adrāka mā laylatul qadr

And what can make you know what (the) Night (of) Power (is)?

لَيْلَةُ الْقَدْرِ خَيْرٌ مِّنْ أَلْفِ شَهْرٍ

Laylatul qadri khayrum min alfi shahr

(The) Night (of) Power (is) better than a thousand months.

تَنَزَّلُ الْمَلَائِكَةُ وَالرُّوحُ فِيهَا بِإِذْنِ رَبِّهِم مِّن كُلِّ أَمْرٍ

Tanazzalul malāikatu war rūḥu fīhā bi idhni rabbihim min kulli amr

Descend the Angels and the Spirit therein, by (the) permission (of) their Nurturer, for every affair.

سَلَامٌ هِيَ حَتَّىٰ مَطْلَعِ الْفَجْرِ

salāmun hiya ḥattā maṭlaʿil fajr

Peace it (is) until (the) emergence (of) the dawn.

2nd *rakʿah*

- Perform the *rukūʿ* and the two *sajdahs*
- Finish the prayer as usual with *tashahhud* and *taslīm*

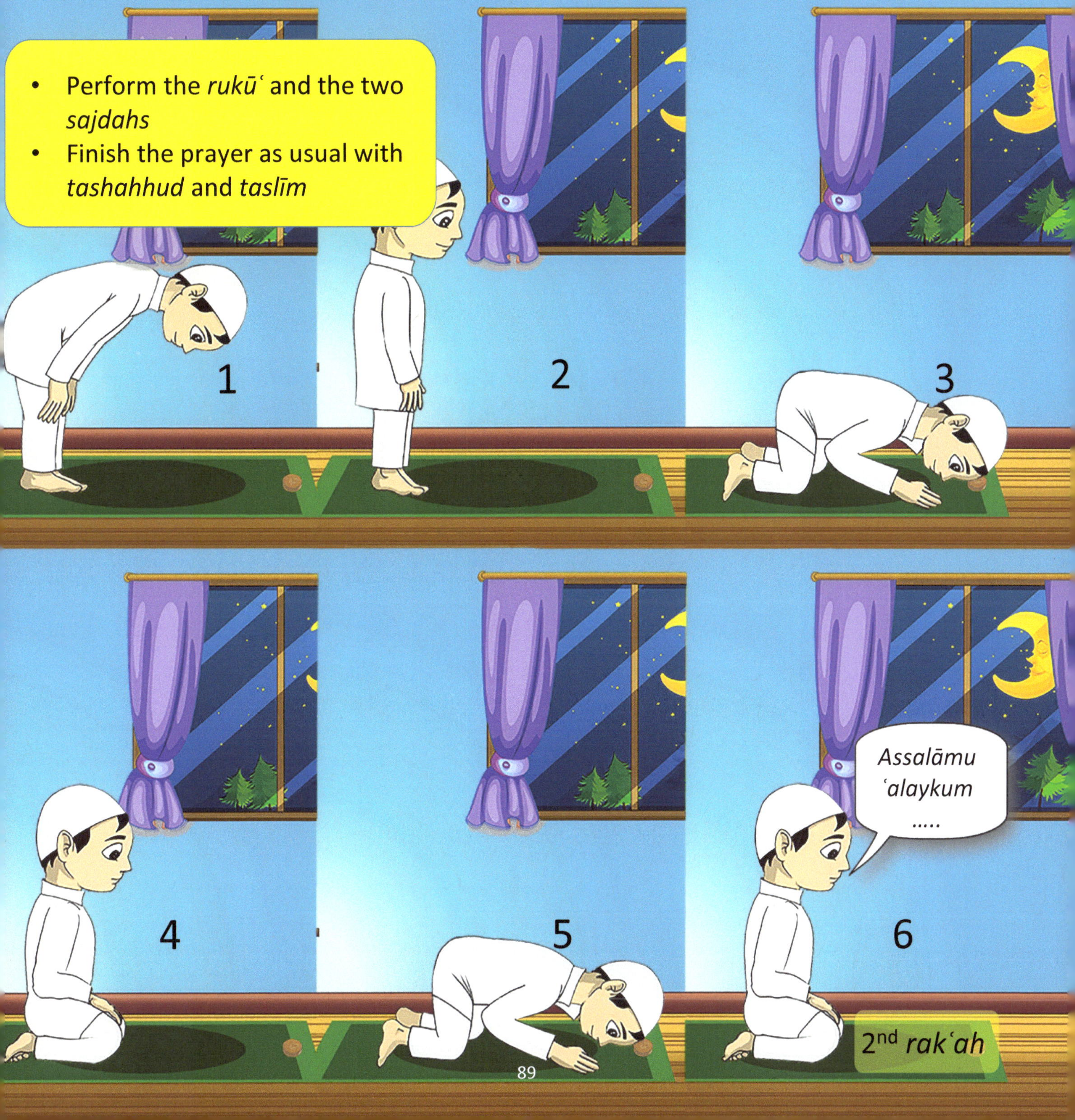

- After the prayer is complete say the following dua
- After that, one should say the name of the deceased person

اَللّٰهُمَّ صَلِّ عَلَىٰ مُحَمَّدٍ وَآلِ مُحَمَّدٍ، وَٱبْعَثْ ثَوَابَهَا إِلَىٰ قَبْرِ-------

Allāhumma ṣalli ʿalā muḥammadi*(n)****w wa āli muḥammad, wabʿath thawābahā ilā qabri*** *(name the deceased)*

O Allah! Bless Muḥammad and the progeny of Muḥammad, and send the reward of this [prayer] to the grave of *(name the deceased).*

Translations

Al-Kursī verses

اَللَّـهُ لَا إِلَـٰهَ إِلَّا هُوَ الْحَيُّ الْقَيُّومُ لَا تَأْخُذُهُ سِنَةٌ وَلَا نَوْمٌ لَّهُ مَا فِي السَّمَاوَاتِ وَمَا فِي الْأَرْضِ مَن ذَا الَّذِي يَشْفَعُ عِندَهُ إِلَّا
بِإِذْنِهِ يَعْلَمُ مَا بَيْنَ أَيْدِيهِمْ وَمَا خَلْفَهُمْ وَلَا يُحِيطُونَ بِشَيْءٍ مِّنْ عِلْمِهِ إِلَّا بِمَا شَاءَ وَسِعَ كُرْسِيُّهُ السَّمَاوَاتِ وَالْأَرْضَ وَلَا يَئُودُهُ
حِفْظُهُمَا وَهُوَ الْعَلِيُّ الْعَظِيمُ (٢٥٥) لَا إِكْرَاهَ فِي الدِّينِ قَد تَّبَيَّنَ الرُّشْدُ مِنَ الْغَيِّ فَمَن يَكْفُرْ بِالطَّاغُوتِ وَيُؤْمِن بِاللَّـهِ فَقَدِ
اسْتَمْسَكَ بِالْعُرْوَةِ الْوُثْقَىٰ لَا انفِصَامَ لَهَا وَاللَّـهُ سَمِيعٌ عَلِيمٌ (٢٥٦) اللَّـهُ وَلِيُّ الَّذِينَ آمَنُوا يُخْرِجُهُم مِّنَ الظُّلُمَاتِ إِلَى النُّورِ
وَالَّذِينَ كَفَرُوا أَوْلِيَاؤُهُمُ الطَّاغُوتُ يُخْرِجُونَهُم مِّنَ النُّورِ إِلَى الظُّلُمَاتِ أُولَـٰئِكَ أَصْحَابُ النَّارِ هُمْ فِيهَا خَالِدُونَ (٢٥٧)

Allah (is He who) there is no god except Him, the Absolute-Ever living, the Self-Existing (while others exist by relying on Him). Drowsiness or sleep do not affect Him. Whatever is in the Skies and whatever is in (or on) the earth belong to Him. No one may intercede with Him (for others) except by His Will. He knows everything about what is evident to people and whatever is hidden from them. However, they cannot comprehend His Knowledge apart from what He Wishes (for them to know). His Authority encompasses the Skies and the Earth, nevertheless, preserving them does not cause Him any difficulty. And He is the Most-High and the Greatest. 2:255

There is no compulsion in (accepting) the religion. Certainly, the (path of) guidance is (clearly) distinct from the (path of) misguidance. So, whoever rejects the false deities and believes in Allah has certainly grasped the strongest handle that never breaks. And Allah is All-Hearing, All-Knowing. 2:256

Allah is the Guardian of those who have believed. He brings them out of the darkness into the Light. And those who deny the Truth, their guardian is the false deities who takes them out of the Light into the darkness. They are the residents of Hell where they will be forever. 2:257

How to Pray The Nawāfil Prayers

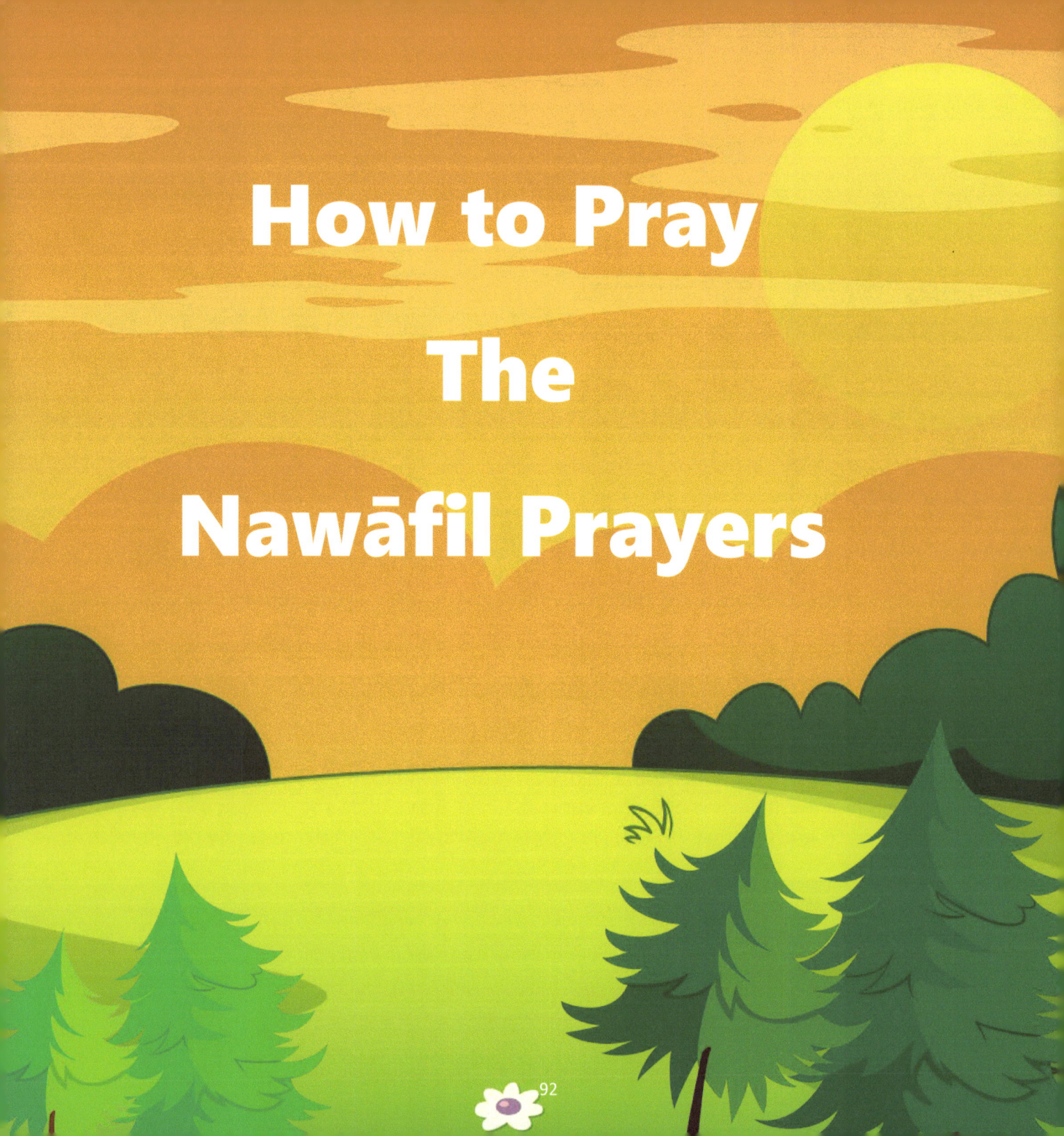

Nawāfil prayers are recommended prayers which have many rewards. There are some leniencies in these prayers; things that are not present in obligatory prayers such as:

1. You can perform the recommended prayers standing or sitting.
2. You can recite Sūrat al-Fātiḥah alone and then go to *rukūʿ*.
3. If you have a doubt in any *rakʿah* it does not invalidate your prayer.
4. These prayers can be performed while walking with no need to face the *qibla*. You can just do a gesture for *rukūʿ* such as bending the head and bending slightly further for *sujud*.

These daily *Nawāfil* prayers are prayed in sets of 2 *rakʿahs* just like *Fajr* prayer.

The *Nāfilah* of *Fajr* prayer has 2 *rakʿahs* and it begins at the false dawn before you pray the *Fajr* prayer. The false dawn being a light, which appears before the true dawn, that moves upwards instead of spreading across the horizon. The true dawn is when a dim, white light which spreads across the horizon and becomes more intensely illuminated as time passes. It is permissible to perform the *Nāfilah* of *Fajr* with the night prayer before false fajr, even at midnight.

The *Nāfilah* of *Ẓuhr* prayer has 8 *rakʿahs*, This means 4 prayers with 2 *rakʿahs* in each prayer. It is performed before you pray the *Ẓuhr* prayer.

The *Nāfilah* of *ʿAṣr* prayer has 8 *rakʿahs*. This means 4 prayers with 2 *rakʿahs* in each prayer. It is performed before *ʿAṣr* prayer.

The *Nāfilah* of *Maghrib* prayer has 4 *rakʿahs*. This means 2 prayers with 2 *rakʿahs* in each prayer. It is performed after *Maghrib* prayer.

The *Nāfilah* of *ʿIshāʾ* prayer has 2 *rakʿahs* and is performed after the *ʿIshāʾ* prayer. But these 2 *rakʿahs* must be performed sitting.

The *Nāfilah* of *Layl* (night) has 11 *rakʿahs*.
The first 8 *rakʿahs* are called *Nāfilah* of *Layl*. So that is 4 prayers with 2 *rakʿahs* in each prayer.
The next 2 *rakʿahs* are called the *Shafʿ* prayer.
And the last 1 *rakʿah* prayer is called the *Witr* prayer.
The best time to pray these prayers is between Midnight and *Fajr*, the closer to *Fajr* the better.

Note: On Fridays, 4 extra *rakʿahs* are added to the 16 *rakʿahs* of *Ẓuhr* and *ʿAṣr* prayers.

Nāfilah of Fajr:
Before *Fajr* prayer
2 *rakʿahs*
Nāfilah of Ẓuhr:
Before *Ẓuhr* prayer
8 *rakʿahs* (4x2)
Nāfilah of ʿAṣr:
Before *ʿAṣr* prayer
8 *rakʿahs* (4x2)
Nāfilah of Maghrib:
After *Maghrib* prayer
4 *rakʿahs* (2x2)
Nāfilah of ʿIshāʾ:
After *ʿIshāʾ* prayer
2 *rakʿahs* (sitting)
Nāfilah of Layl:
Best time closest to *Fajr* time
11 *rakʿahs*

How to Pray Nāfilah of ʿIshāʾ prayer

2 x *rakʿahs* sitting

- After you have finished your *ʿIshāʾ* prayer, remain seated
- Make your intention
- Perform *Takbīrat al-iḥrām*

- Remain seated
- Recite Sūrah al-Fātiḥah
- Now recite another *Sūrah* if preferred

1st *rakʿah*

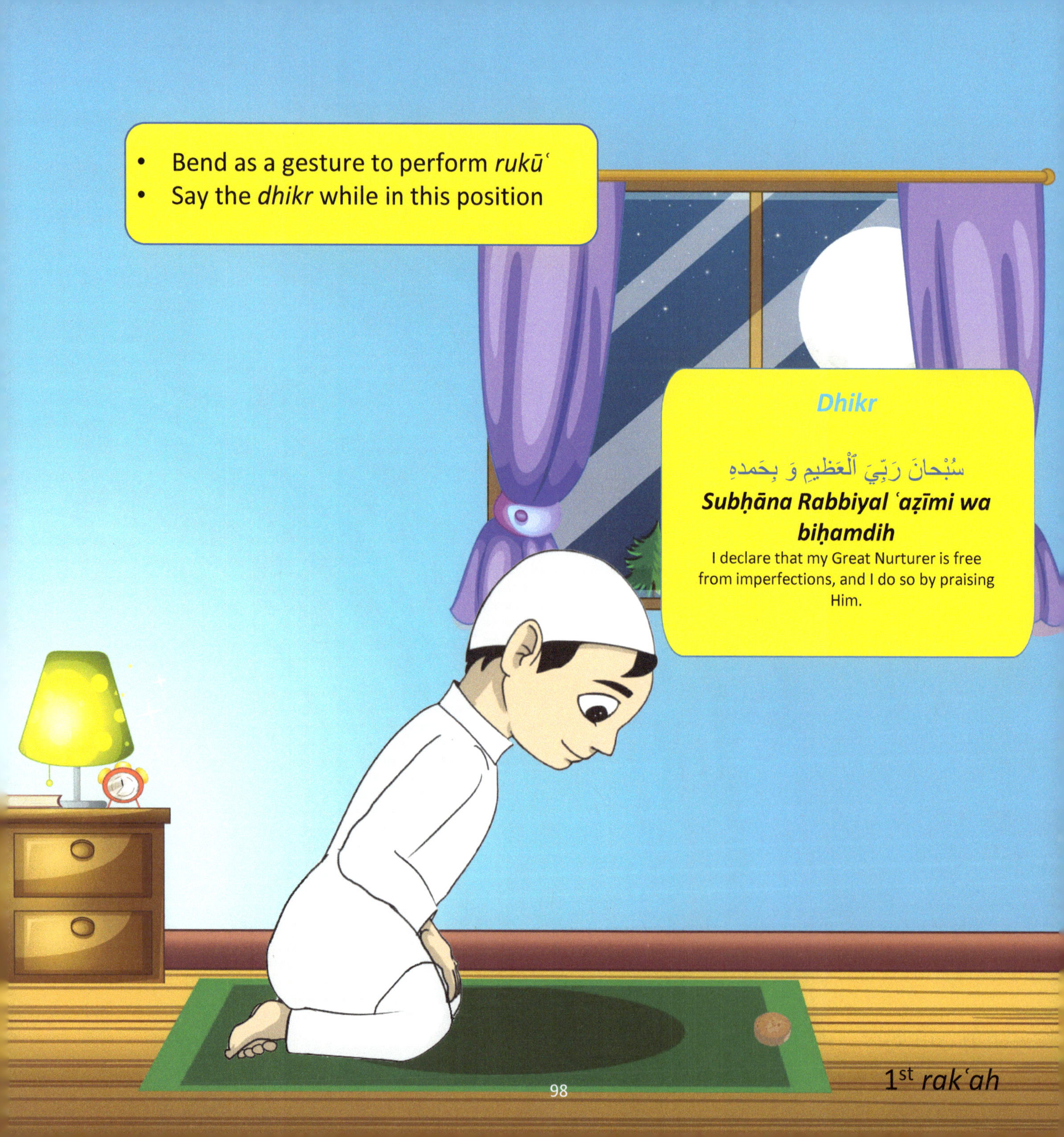

- Bend as a gesture to perform *rukūʿ*
- Say the *dhikr* while in this position

Dhikr

سُبْحانَ رَبِّيَ ٱلْعَظِيمِ وَ بِحَمدهِ

Subḥāna Rabbiyal ʿaẓīmi wa biḥamdih

I declare that my Great Nurturer is free from imperfections, and I do so by praising Him.

1st *rakʿah*

Sit back up and say the *takbīr*

1st *rak'ah*

Perform the two *sajdahs* and *dhikr* as normal
1
2
3
4
1st *rak'ah*

- Remain seated
- Do the same as the first *rakʿah*
- Finish the prayer as usual with *tashahhud* and *taslīm*

2nd *rakʿah*

How to Pray Nāfilah of Layl

8 x *rakʿahs* (4 x 2 *rakʿahs*)

Nafilah of Layl

- Make your intention
- Perform *Takbīrat al-iḥrām*

- Recite Sūrah al-Fātiḥah
- Then recite Sūrah al-Ikhlāṣ once

بِسْمِ اللَّـهِ الرَّحْمَـٰنِ الرَّحِيمِ

Bismil lāhir Raḥmānir Raḥīm

I start in the name of Allah, The All-Merciful, The Kindest towards believers.

قُلْ هُوَ اللَّـهُ أَحَدٌ

Qul huwal lāhu aḥad

Say, He is Allah, the One.

اللَّـهُ الصَّمَدُ

Allahuṣ Ṣamad

Allah is Who is independent of all beings.

لَمْ يَلِدْ وَلَمْ يُولَدْ

Lam yalid wa lam yūlad

He has never had an offspring, nor was He born.

وَلَمْ يَكُن لَّهُ كُفُوًا أَحَدٌ

Wa lam yaku(n)l lahu kufuwan aḥad

Nor has He any equal.

1st *rakʿah*

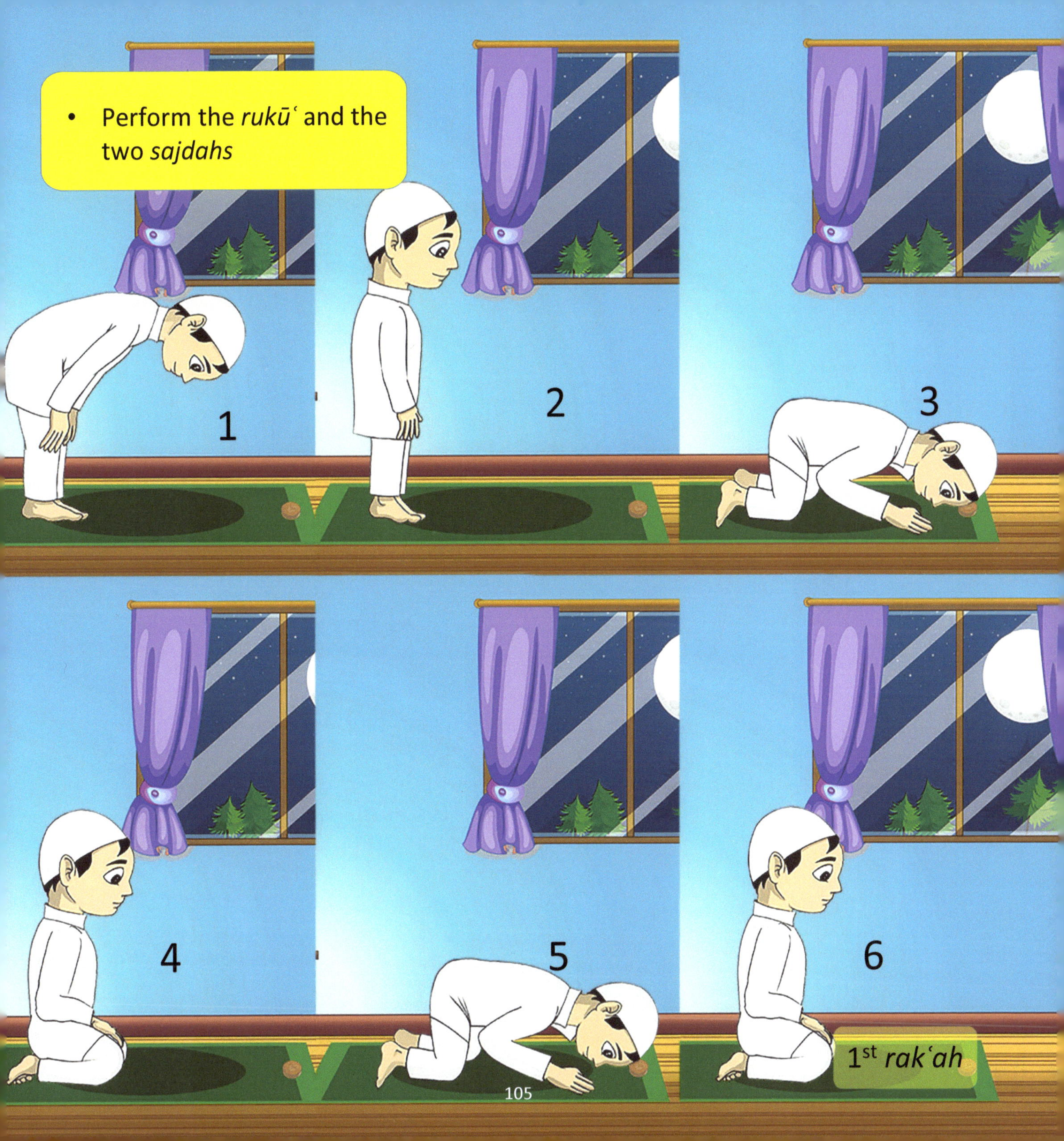
• Perform the *rukūʿ* and the two *sajdahs*
1
2
3
4
5
6
1st *rakʿah*

- Stand back up for the second *rakʿah*
- Recite Sūrah al-Fātiḥah
- Then recite Sūrah al-Kāfirūn once

بِسْمِ اللَّـهِ الرَّحْمَـٰنِ الرَّحِيمِ

Bismil lāhir Raḥmānir Raḥīm

I start in the name of Allah, The All-Merciful, The Kindest towards believers.

قُلْ يَٰٓأَيُّهَا ٱلْكَٰفِرُونَ

Qul yā ayyuhal kāfirūn

Say, O disbelievers,

لَآ أَعْبُدُ مَا تَعْبُدُونَ

Lā aʿbudu mā taʿbudūn

I do not worship what you worship.

وَلَا أَنتُمْ عَابِدُونَ مَا أَعْبُدُ

Walā antum ʿābidūna mā aʿbud

Nor are you worshippers of what I worship.

وَلَآ أَنَا۠ عَابِدٌ مَّا عَبَدتُّمْ

Walā ana ʿābidu(n)m mā ʿabattum

Nor will I be a worshipper of what you worship.

وَلَا أَنتُمْ عَابِدُونَ مَا أَعْبُدُ

Walā antum ʿābidūna mā aʿbud

Nor will you be worshippers of what I worship.

لَكُمْ دِينُكُمْ وَلِىَ دِينِ

Lakum dīnukum waliya dīn

For you is your religion, and for me is my religion.

2nd *rakʿah*

- It is recommended to perform *qunūt* and recite all your needs if preferred
- It is sufficient to say *Subḥān Allah* 3 times

Qunūt

سُبْحَانَ اللهِ

***Subḥān Allah* x 3**

I declare that Allah is free from imperfections.

2nd *rakʿah*

- Perform the *rukūʿ* and the two *sajdahs*
- Finish the prayer as usual with *tashahhud* and *taslīm*
- **Repeat this prayer 4 times all up**

How to Pray The Shafʿ Prayer

2 x *rakʿahs*

The Shafʿ Prayer

- Make your intention
- Perform *Takbīrat al-iḥrām*

- Recite Sūrah al-Fātiḥah
- Then recite Sūrah al-Nās once

بِسْمِ اللَّهِ الرَّحْمَٰنِ الرَّحِيمِ

Bismil lāhir Raḥmānir Raḥīm

I start in the name of Allah, The All-Merciful, The Kindest towards believers.

قُلْ أَعُوذُ بِرَبِّ ٱلنَّاسِ

Qul aʿūdhu bi rabbin nās

Say, I seek protection with the Nurturer of all the people.

مَلِكِ ٱلنَّاسِ

Malikin nās

The King of all the people.

إِلَٰهِ ٱلنَّاسِ

Ilāhin nās

The God of all the people.

مِن شَرِّ ٱلْوَسْوَاسِ ٱلْخَنَّاسِ

Min sharril waswāsil khannās

From the evil of the retreating whisperer.

ٱلَّذِى يُوَسْوِسُ فِى صُدُورِ ٱلنَّاسِ

Alladhī yuwaswisu fī ṣudūrin nās

The one who whispers [evil] into the hearts of the people.

مِنَ ٱلْجِنَّةِ وَٱلنَّاسِ

Minal jinnati wan nās

From among the jinn and the people.

1st *rakʿah*

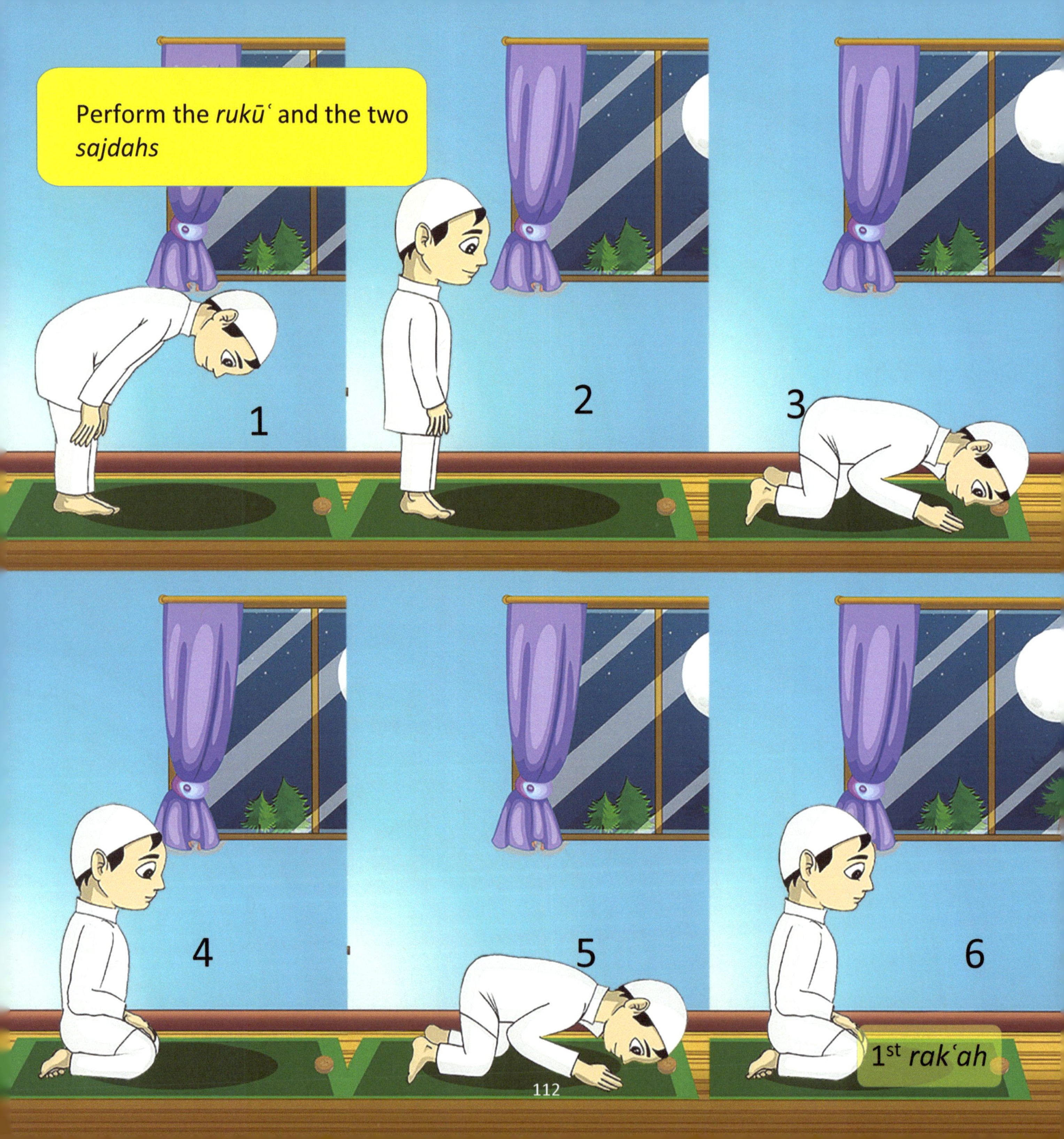
Perform the *rukūʿ* and the two *sajdahs*
1
2
3
4
5
6
1st *rakʿah*

- Stand back up for the second *rakʿah*
- Recite Sūrah al-Fātiḥah
- Then recite Sūrah al-Falaq once

بِسْمِ اللَّهِ الرَّحْمَٰنِ الرَّحِيمِ

Bismil lāhir Raḥmānir Raḥīm

I start in the name of Allah, The All-Merciful, The Kindest towards believers.

قُلْ أَعُوذُ بِرَبِّ الْفَلَقِ

Qul aʿūdhu bi rabbil falaq

Say: I seek protection with the Nurturer of the Daybreak.

مِن شَرِّ مَا خَلَقَ

Min sharri mā khalaq

From the evil of which He has created.

وَمِن شَرِّ غَاسِقٍ إِذَا وَقَبَ

Wa min sharri ghāsiqin idhā waqab

And from the evil of the dark night when it comes.

وَمِن شَرِّ النَّفَّاثَاتِ فِي الْعُقَدِ

Wa min sharrin nafāthāti fīl ʿuqad

And from the evil of those who blow on knots.

وَمِن شَرِّ حَاسِدٍ إِذَا حَسَدَ

Wa min sharri ḥāsidin idhā ḥasad

And from the evil of the envious (ones) when they envy.

2nd *rakʿah*

- Perform the *rukūʿ* and the two *sajdahs*
- Finish the prayer as usual with *tashahhud* and *taslīm*

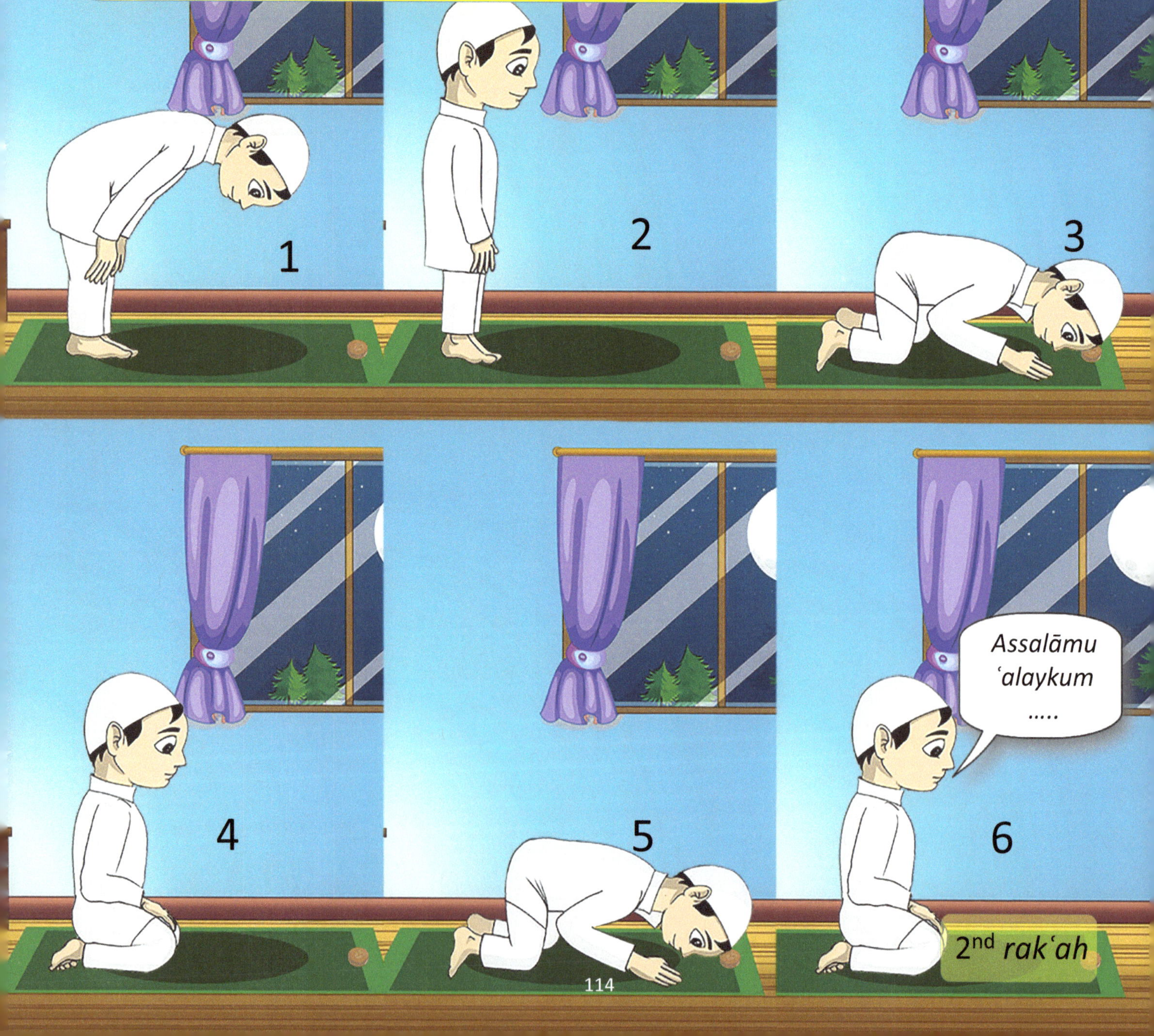

How to Pray The Witr Prayer

1 x *rakʿah*

The Witr Prayer

- Make your intention
- Perform *Takbīrat al-iḥrām*

- Recite Sūrah al-Fātiḥah
- Then recite Sūrah al-Ikhlāṣ once or three times

بِسْمِ اللَّـهِ الرَّحْمَـٰنِ الرَّحِيمِ

Bismil lāhir Raḥmānir Raḥīm

I start in the name of Allah, The All-Merciful, The Kindest towards believers.

قُلْ هُوَ اللَّـهُ أَحَدٌ

Qul huwal lāhu aḥad

Say, He is Allah, the One.

اللَّـهُ الصَّمَدُ

Allahuṣ Ṣamad

Allah is Who is independent of all beings.

لَمْ يَلِدْ وَلَمْ يُولَدْ

Lam yalid wa lam yūlad

He has never had an offspring, nor was He born.

وَلَمْ يَكُن لَّهُ كُفُوًا أَحَدٌ

Wa lam yaku(n)l lahu kufuwan aḥad

Nor has He any equal.

Now recite Sūrah al-Falaq once

Sūrah al-Falaq

بِسْمِ اللَّهِ الرَّحْمَٰنِ الرَّحِيمِ

Bismil lāhir Raḥmānir Raḥīm
I start in the name of Allah, The All-Merciful, The Kindest towards believers.

قُلْ أَعُوذُ بِرَبِّ ٱلْفَلَقِ

Qul aʿūdhu bi rabbil falaq
Say: I seek protection with the Nurturer of the Daybreak.

مِن شَرِّ مَا خَلَقَ

Min sharri mā khalaq
From the evil of which He has created.

وَمِن شَرِّ غَاسِقٍ إِذَا وَقَبَ

Wa min sharri ghāsiqin idhā waqab
And from the evil of the dark night when it comes.

وَمِن شَرِّ النَّفَّاثَاتِ فِي الْعُقَدِ

Wa min sharrin-nafāthāti fīl ʿuqad
And from the evil of those who blow on knots.

وَمِن شَرِّ حَاسِدٍ إِذَا حَسَدَ

Wa min sharri ḥāsidin idhā ḥasad
And from the evil of the envious (ones) when they envy.

Now recite Sūrah al-Nās once

بِسْمِ اللَّـهِ الرَّحْمَـٰنِ الرَّحِيمِ

Bismil lāhir Raḥmānir Raḥīm

I start in the name of Allah, The All-Merciful, The Kindest towards believers.

قُلْ أَعُوذُ بِرَبِّ ٱلنَّاسِ

Qul aʿūdhu bi rabbin nās

Say, I seek protection with the Nurturer of all the people.

مَلِكِ ٱلنَّاسِ

Malikin nās

The King of all the people.

إِلَـٰهِ ٱلنَّاسِ

Ilāhin nās

The God of all the people.

مِن شَرِّ ٱلْوَسْوَاسِ ٱلْخَنَّاسِ

Min sharril waswāsil khannās

From the evil of the retreating whisperer.

ٱلَّذِى يُوَسْوِسُ فِى صُدُورِ ٱلنَّاسِ

Alladhī yuwaswisu fī ṣudūrin nās

The one who whispers [evil] into the hearts of the people.

مِنَ ٱلْجِنَّةِ وَٱلنَّاسِ

Minal jinnati wan nās

From among the jinn and the people.

- It is recommended to perform *qunūt* and try to weep out of fear of Allah
- There are many supplications one can recite during *qunūt* however we will mention those that are highly advisable

Repeat the following 70 times:

اَسْتَغْفِرُ اللّٰهَ رَبِّي وَ اَتُوْبُ اِلَيْهِ

Astaghfirul lāha rabbī wa a-tūbu ilayh

I seek forgiveness of Allah my Nurturer, and I turn to Him.

Pray for the forgiveness of 40 people

Repeat the following 40 times:

اَللّٰهُمَّ اغْفِرْ لِ ....

Allahummagh firli... (Name a person)

O Allah, forgive (Name a person)...

Apart from relatives and friends, it is recommended to remember the scholars who have served and propagated Islam. If it is not possible to name forty believers, name as many as possible and then say:

اَللّٰهُمَّ اغْفِرْ لِلْمُؤْمِنِيْنَ وَ الْمُؤْمِنَاتِ

Allahummagh fir lil muʾminīna wal muʾmināt

O Allah forgive all believers, male and female.

Then it is recommended to say the following:

Repeat the following 7 times:

هٰذَا مَقَامُ الْعَآئِذِ بِكَ مِنَ النَّارِ

Hādhā maqāmul ʿā-idhi bika minan nār

This is the position of one who seeks refuge in You from the fire [of Hell].

Then Repeat the following 300 times:

اَلْعَفو

Al-aʿfuw

I seek Your pardon.

Then Repeat the following once:

رَبِّ اغْفِرْ لِي وَ ارْحَمْنِي وَ تُبْ عَلَيَّ اِنَّكَ اَنْتَ التَّوَّابُ الرَّحِيْمُ

Rabbighfirlī warḥamnī wa tub ʿalayya innaka antat tawwābur raḥīm

(O my) Nurturer, forgive me and have mercy on me, and turn to me. Indeed, You are the Oft-returning, the Merciful.

- Perform the *rukūʿ* and the two *sajdahs*
- Finish the prayer as usual with *tashahhud* and *taslīm*

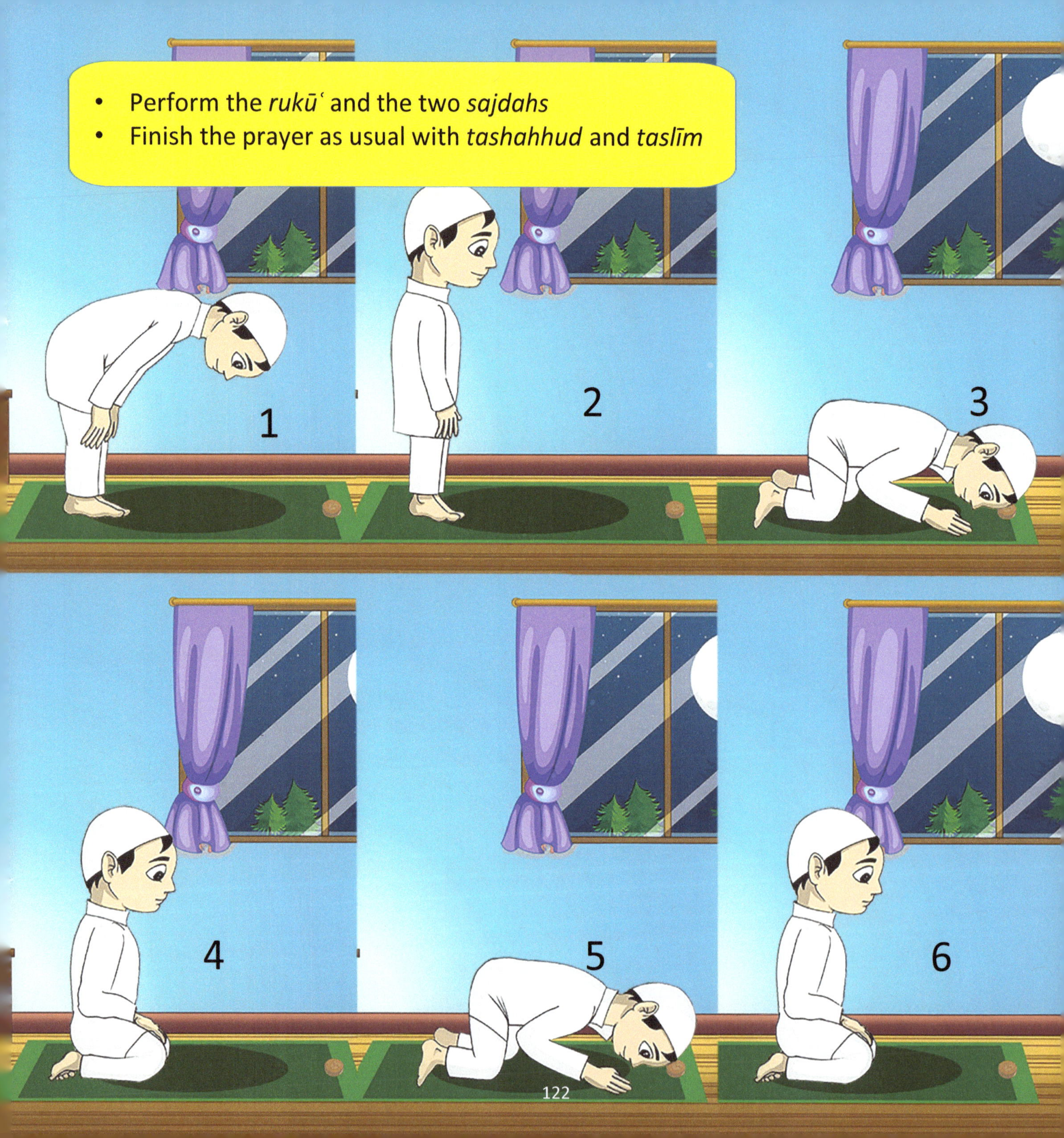

Glossary

Dhikr - Remembrance

Dua - Supplication

Eid al-Aḍḥā - Festival of Sacrifice

Eid al-Fiṭr - Festival of Breaking the Fast

Kursī - Throne

Layl - Night

Masjid al-Ḥarām - The Sacred Mosque

Nawāfil - Voluntary

Qibla - Direction that Muslims face

Qunūt - Humility in certain position

Rakʿah - Unit of prayer

Rukūʿ - Bowing

Sajdah - Prostration

Ṣalāt al-ʿAṣr - Afternoon prayer

Ṣalāt al-Fajr - Dawn prayer

Ṣalāt al-ʿIshāʾ - Night prayer

Ṣalāt al-Maghrib - Evening prayer

Ṣalāt al-Shafʿ - 2 *rakʿah* night prayer

Ṣalāt al-Witr - 1 *rakʿah* night prayer

Ṣalāt al-Ẓuhr - Midday prayer

Sūrah - Chapter

Takbīr - Allahu Akbar

Takbīrat al-iḥrām - The opening *Takbīr*

Tasbiḥ - Glorification

Tashahhud - Testifying

Taslīm - Salutation

Zakāt al-fiṭrah - Charity of Fasting

Credit

All praise belongs to Allah, the All Merciful towards all existents, the Kindest towards believers. He Who has given us enough patience and courage to complete this book.

Islamic Lessons Made Easy would like to thank all those involved in this project for their hard work and commitment.

EDITORS

Amir Hussein

Kawthar Ibrahim

Sheikh Dr Zaid Alsalami

اللّهُمَّ صَلِّ عَلَى مُحَمّدٍ وَآلِ مُحَمّدٍ

Allahumma ṣalli ʿala Muḥammadi(n)w wa āli Muḥammad

O Allah, (please do) bless Muḥammad and the Household of Muḥammad

Contact : Admin@islamiclessonsmadeeasy.com.au

Visit us :

Facebook.com/islamiclessonsmadeeasy

Youtube.com/islamiclessonsmadeeasy

Instagram.com/islamic_lessons_me

Islamiclessonsmadeeasy.com.au

Ilme.net.au

www.ingramcontent.com/pod-product-compliance
Lightning Source LLC
Chambersburg PA
CBHW041102070526
44583CB00002B/29
9781764084277